SS ARMOR

A Pictorial History of the Armored Formations of the Waffen-SS

by Robert C. Stern

illustrated by Don Greer and Ron Volstad

squadron/signal publications

Author's Note

This book came into being as the direct consequence of th
discovery of a previously unpublished group of SS photograph
among the resources of the Bundesarchiv, Koblenz. While some
the photos are not of the best quality, the unique opportunity t
put these and others from Squadron/Signal's archives into print
and to update and supplement the previous "Waffen SS in Action
at the same time, demanded immediate action. It is not m
intention here to write a definitive history of the SS, as man
other books explore that subject in great depth. It is, however, m
definite intention to explore by use of these photographs, th
evolution and use of SS armor, its camouflage and markings.

The unfortunate fact with which any researcher has to de
when studying SS armor is that nearly all the photographs dat
from a fairly brief mid-war period. Earlier on, there was no offici
SS armor, and later, when the tide had turned, few photos wer
taken and fewer still have survived. To partially overcome th
deficit, I have at times liberally interpreted "armored" a
"motorized" allowing the inclusion of some vehicles from unit
before they were officially armored and others that were neve
officially armored.

The format of this book is basically chronological. The story o
the SS motorized and armored units in World War II seem
naturally to fall into four periods, which are the basis fo
"chapters" in this book. The text has been kept short, giving only
brief synopsis of events, because it is hoped that the maps an
photographs, with their captions, will present the substance o
this book in the most useful form.

Note: All maps in this book show political boundaries as of 1939

Acknowledgements

I would like to thank Tom Ferris for his expertise on the
uniforms and equipment of the SS; Scott Van Ness whose research
has been invaluable.

This book is dedicated to Pat for her love and patience, and
Erci with hope that it will be nothing more than a picture book.

Photo Credits

Bundesarchiv Koblenz
US Army
National Archives
Public Archives Canada
Scott Van Ness

ISBN 0-89747-066-4

[Cover] A PzKpfw III ausf J and PzKpfw II ausf F of Leibstandarte
advance into a Central Russian town on the way to Belgorod during
the Manstein Offensive, March 1944.

Introduction

The story of SS Armor begins with the Polish Campaign of 1939, although the first official SS Panzer regiment did not come into existence until Spring 1942. And even prior to that, the temporary SS groups that did exist were all motorized to a far greater extent than their Army counterparts. The armored support groups that were normally assigned to motorized infantry regiments, such as Reconaissance and Panzerjäger detachments, began to be assembled during the summer of 1939, some seeing combat in Poland.

Our story thereafter is primarily concerned with the four main SS divisions that were in existence at the time of Barbarossa, both because they were the most active, and because they are the most fully documented. We follow their rise to the point, that in July 1943, the SS-Panzer-Korps (containing three of these divisions) may well have been the most awesome armor grouping of its kind ever assembled, massing over 1,000 armored vehicles. We then follow the decline of these and the newer SS armored units as they tried to stem the overwhelming Allied tide. In each battle losing more than could be replaced, they eventually surrendered as mere shadows of their former strength.

Much has been written about the elite status of SS units, some of it true. What is undeniable is that, elite or not, the Waffen SS tended to be better equipped than other German units. They would receive new equipment first and be supplied with replacements of both equipment and personnel more frequently. This could not help but make them more effective in combat. Nor in portraying the Waffen SS can it be forgotten that their ranks were drawn, at least at first, from politically pure Nazi believers, with all that implies of national, political and racial hatred. It is not surprising that these men soon acquired a reputation for brutality beyond that necessary in warfare. While less directly implicated than other SS establishments, and no more so than many army units, the Waffen SS tarnished their warrior image by involvement in numerous attrocities, from assisting in the massive slaughter of Jews, Russians, Poles and others in the East to the relatively petty barbarities, such as Malmedy, in the West. The Waffen SS was not involved in the planning, and only marginally in the staffing, of the concentration camps. Yet, any attempt to portray the Waffen SS as clean while others were committing the crimes simply does not withstand truthful examination. Perhaps most truthfully, it can be stated that the fighting branches of the SS took the qualities of the German soldier to its extremes. At times brutal, they could also be extraordinarily brave and resourceful, seemingly most often against tremendous odds.

Armored Warfare! The "co-ordination of arms" preached by Guderian, the key to the success of German armor, could hardly be more clearly shown than in this photograph of Leibstandarte **at Kursk. Although only one tank is visible [a PzBefWg III silhouetted against the sky on the right], the view gives a good idea of the numbers and kinds of vehicles required by a mechanized unit. At the crest of the ravine an anti-tank detachment is digging in, five SdKfz 10 one ton halftracks being visible, while the command group is prudently sited at the bottom of the ravine mounted on three Kfz 70 Horch mPkws and a single Kfz 1/20 VW Schwimmwagen. Meanwhile, a reconnaissance unit is crossing their front under the protection of the far ridge with an even dozen SdKfz 250s, while the command tank and an additional 250, probably from regimental HQ, view the scene from atop the ridge. Those vehicles on which camouflage can be ascertained appear to be in overall Panzer Grey or Sand Yellow with Red Brown overspray, this being a transitional period. [Scott Van Ness]**

Development: Fall 1939-Spring 1942

Between the beginning of hostilities in September 1939 and the Summer of 1942 the armored units of the Waffen SS came into existence. In response to the demands for an increasing mobilization of the nation, this period of less than three years saw expansion and strengthening of the mechanized SS troops far exceeding that of the previous ten. At the beginning of this period, the Waffen SS was comprised of several independent standarten (regiments), and a few motorized support units. Some of these were intended to be joined into a motorized division at some future date. And even this level of organization had only been reached through the efforts of a retired army officer. Yet by the Summer of 1942, the Waffen SS was composed of six full divisions, four of those having just received two battalion Panzer Regiments that made each of them more than equivalent in strength to any Wehrmacht Panzer Division.

The SS had been in existence since before 1923 but did not officially differentiate its military branch from the police and security sections until 1933 when the SS-Verfungungstruppen (SS-VT=Special Purpose Troops) were gradually defined. These included the **Stabswache** (Hitler's Bodyguard). The **Stabswache**, after an intervening reorganization, was officially renamed **Leibstandarte SS Adolf Hitler** at the Nurnburg Party Rally in September of that year, under the command of Josef "Sepp" Dietrich. In December 1934, **Leibstandarte** was officially motorized, setting the pattern for later Waffen SS formations.

The continuing desire on the part of the SS to field combat formations to rival those of the newly re-born Wehrmacht led to the announcement in March 1935 that an SS-Division would be formed from various SS-VT units. After more than a year had passed and little significant progress had been made toward that goal, the SS retained the services of Paul Hausser, a retired Army General-leutnant. Hausser knew he had his work cut out for him, taking the loosely organized regional formations of the SS-VT, molding them into the tightly disciplined grenadier standarten and auxilliary groupings essential to a crack division. The first requirement he laid down was that all elements of the division were to be entirely motorized, meaning that the future **SS-V-Division** would be a mobile, as well as elite, formation. Over the next two years Hausser oversaw the establishment of the second and third motorized Standarten, **Deutschland [D]** and **Germania [G]**.

Because of the political as well as military character of the early SS military formations, they were often put in the most visible positions during Germany's pre-war muscleflexing. In March 1936, **Leibstandarte [LAH]** was the first unit to cross into the re-militarized Rheinland, entering triumphantly (and photogenically) into Saarbrucken. Exactly two years later, **LAH** again led the way, this time as the spearhead of Guderian's XVI Armee during the Anschluss. Immediately following this occupation of Austria, the fourth Standarte **Der Fuhrer [DF]**, composed of Austrian Nazis, began to assemble. A year and a half later this regiment was not ready for combat, so it was with the original three SS Standarten [**LAH D & G**], those SS-VT divisional troops who had been assembled to this point, and a few assorted battalion-size Totenkopfverbande (units formed to give military experience to concentration camp guards) that the SS went to war.

The SS units that were available for the Polish Campaign were not used as a group but were split up, **LAH** being assigned to the 11. Armee-Korps of 10. Armee (H-Gr Süd) while **Germania** was placed into H-Gr Süd reserve. Both travelled considerable distance and saw some fighting. **Deutschland** had an even more exciting time of it. Along with a number of Army units, **D** (together with SS-VT divisional troops) had been transported to East Prussia in June 1939. There it was ostensibly to participate in a massed parade at the Tannenberg memorial and take part in maneuvers. Among the formations

also in East Prussia was 4. Panzer-Brigade, composed of 7. and 8. Panzer-Regiments (later to form the armored elements of 10. Panzer-Division). In order to give von Küchler's 3. Armee something equivalent to the Panzer Divisions massed elsewhere on the Polish border, **Deutschland** was joined to the 4. Panzer-Brigade and SS-VT Reconnaissance and Artillery Battalions (SS-Auf-Abt and SS-Art-Abt) to form the ad hoc formation, Panzer-Verband Ostpreussen. 1. Armee-Korps, of which Pz-Verb Ostpr was part, served as the left wing of the German advance into Poland, eventually participating in the capture of Brest-Litovsk.

Upon the successful completion of the Polish Campaign, and with the unpleasant realization that the Allies were not going to sue for peace, the German armed forces began a feverish expansion and reorganization. This was especially true of Waffen-SS which had proved itself in Poland to be brave but at times poorly organized and led.

The already authorized **SS-VT-Division [mot]** was hurriedly assembled and began intensive training. Two new SS divisions were authorized in October 1939 which also began rapid assembly. The **SS-Totenkopf-Division [SS-T]** was formed around the nucleus of the camp guard battalions that saw action in Poland. The **Polizei-Division [Pol]**, composed of Ordnungspolizei, an already semi-military branch of the national police, was organized at the same time. It was always the weakest of Waffen-SS divisions. Not being composed of politically and racially pure party members, the **Polizei-Division** was never favored to the same extent as other Waffen-SS divisions, receiving captured or obsolescent weapons and not being motorized until 1943. In fact, it was February 1942 before its police uniforms were traded in for those of the Waffen-SS and that is name was changed to **SS-Polizei-Division**. None of the SS units took part in the invasion of Denmark and Norway, but by May 1940, the Waffen-SS, now comprising three divisions (two motorized) and a strong regiment, was ready again for action.

The disposition of Waffen-SS troops for the French Campaign was again designed for maximum visibility. **Leibstandarte** and **SS-T** were in Army Reserve at the beginning of action, though the motorcycle battalion of **LAH** was positioned in the front ranks intended to race ahead of other ground units to Rotterdam to link up with Kurt Student's Fallschirmjäger. The **SS-Verfugungdivision [SS-V, its name changed from SS-VT in April]** was assigned to 39. Armee-Korps (mot) along with 9. Panzer-Division. **SS-V** saw some fighting almost immediately, becoming involved with fierce local resistance soon after passing into Holland. It was not until nearly two weeks later that the remaining SS units came face to face with the enemy. Coming into action piecemeal along the southern edge of the Dunkirk salient of trapped British and French troops. They took over frontage from Guderian's tired Panzer Divisions. The SS units maintained pressure [**SS-T** along with Rommel's 7. Panzer-Division fighting off a major Allied armored counterattack at Arras, 21-22 May], but as was the case with the rest of the German forces, were unable to press hard enough to prevent the evacuations from Dunkirk.

With the completion of the first half of the French Campaign, all German Forces were again reorganized and moved into position on the Somme-Aisne line. **SS-T** moved into Army Reserve seeing no more serious fighting, being used to mop up pockets of resistance behind the advancing Panzers. Both **Leibstandarte** and **SS-V** were joined with the Army's 9. and 10. Panzer-Divisions in 14. Armee-Korps(mot) at Amiens. The second phase of the French Campaign began on 5 June 1940. Attacking south from the Amiens bridgehead, von Kleist's 14. Korps met only limited success. So fierce was French resistance at this point that, after two days of negligible advance, the corps was withdrawn and transferred 75 miles to the East. On 11 June, 14. Korps attacked again, this time at Berry-au-Bac, and this time with success. The advance now was rapid, by 14 June the Seine was crossed and orders received to drive on the

Loire to cut the retreat of French units heading for Bordeaux. By 24 June, when the Armistice came into effect, **SS-V** was approaching the Garonne Southwest of Angouleme, having covered more distance than any other German unit. Under the terms of the Armistice, the units of 14. Korps continued to the Spanish frontier to complete the occupation of coastal France.

Immediately after the conquest of France, the Waffen-SS began another period of rapid expansion and reorganization. Both SS motorized divisions and **Leibstandarte** were given training areas in France, to complete at leisure the training that had been interupted by the French Campaign. **SS-T** was assigned to the Biscay coast area just north of the Spanish border where it remained until the end of April 1941. **Leibstandarte** and **SS-V** were both assigned to lead the projected invasion of Britain (Operation "Sealion"), and therefore began intensive amphibious training. **LAH** was the most immediate benefactor of this strengthening process, being raised to brigade status in August though it still retained the title of standarte. In December, a fourth Waffen-SS division was authorized, to be composed of Scandanavian and Dutch volunteers and the standarte **Germania** taken from SS-V. In honor of famous regiment that was to be its core, the new division was named **SS-Division[mot] "Germania"**. To make up for the loss of one of its regiments, **SS-V** was supplied with a newly formed, partially motorized Totenkopf regiment, and at the same time renamed **SS-Division "Deutschland"** after its remaining original standarte. Neither new name was to last very long because of the obvious confusion with the regiments of the same name. At the beginning of January 1941, **Germania** became **SS-Division "Wiking"**. **Wiking** began to gather at Heuberg, being declared combat ready on 1 April 1941. **Deutschland** was renamed **SS-Division "Reich"** at the end of January. With the cancellation of "Sealion" and the decision to intervene in Yugoslavia and Greece, **LAH** and **Reich** were rapidly transferred eastward at the end of March. **LAH** was sent to Kyustendil, Rumania, where it became part of 40. Armee-Korps(mot) along with 9. Panzer-Division, and **Reich** went to Temesvar, also in Rumania, where it joined IR "Grossdeutschland" and Brigade "Hermann Göring" in the truly elite 41. Armee-Korps(mot).

The involvement of SS-Division **Reich** in the Balkan Campaign was brief but intense. As befits the status of the units it contained, 41. Korps was given the task of capturing Belgrade, a process which took only four days. After the capitulation of the Yugoslav capital on 13 April 1941, **Reich** was transferred to Poland in anticipation of the invasion of Russia.

Leibstandarte had a much more prolonged and arduous part to play. Breaking into Southern Yugoslavia on 9 April, **LAH** made contact the next day with the Italian forces that had retreated into Albania, completing the first phase of its task. It then immediately turned south into Greece in a drive that was to take it to southernmost tip of that country. Coming under fire to British forces that same afternoon, **LAH** began a sequence of outflanking maneuvers and frontal attacks in excellent defensive terrain that was to dislodge the Allies from Greece in 18 days. Never allowing the British a chance to establish themselves firmly, **Leibstandarte**, in conjunction with 9. Panzer-Division, forced them out of their positions in Northern Greece. Choosing not to follow the retreat of the Allies through Thermopylae and Corinth, **LAH** drove due south to Mesolongion. Crossing the Gulf of Corinth in fishing boats, **Leibstandarte** arrived on the Peloponnesus at the same time as the retreating British. By 25 April, the British had been forced into a small beachhead at Kalamata. In a pattern similar to Dunkirk, the British fiercely resisted German attack until arriving German reinforcements forced its surrender three days later, after most troops had been evacuated.

The entire Waffen-SS field strength was brought into line for the upcoming invastion of Russia. Hastily refitted (and renamed **SS - Division Leibstandarte - SS "Adolf Hitler"**, but not strenghtened), **LAH** was designated part of 54. Armee-Korps,

while **Wiking** were assigned to von Kleist's Panzer-Gruppe 1, both of Heeres-Gruppe Süd. **Reich** was assigned to Guderian's Panzer-Gruppe 2 of Heeres-Gruppe Mitte, while **Totenkopf** was part of Hoepner's Panzer-Gruppe 4 of Heeres-Gruppe Nord.

None of the SS units saw much action in the first days, all being held in close reserve. **Wiking** came into action first, on 29 June at Tarnopol. Its partner in the South, **Leibstandarte**, was not first blooded until it was used in the abortive attempt by Kurt "Panzer" Meyer's SS-Auf-Abt to storm the Tarter Ditch blocking the entrance to Crimea. **LAH** was then hurriedly transferred to Pz-Gr 1 to participate in the southern half of the massive encirclement of the Kiev Pocket, and remained part of that unit for the drive on Rostov. By mid-November, **LAH** was in the city and **Wiking** just north of it, both heavily pressed by Russian counterattacks. At the end of November, both had been badly mauled by fierce combat, and with the rest of the southern front were pulled back to more secure positions on the Mius. Those positions would be occupied against constant enemy attack until late Spring 1942.

Reich had remained in reserve until 10 July when it was thrown into the fighting at Yelnya on the Desna. Here, at the springboard to Moscow, Pz-Gr 2 held off Russian counterattacks for five weeks, in some of the bloodiest fighting of the war. In late August, however, **Reich** was pulled out of line and moved south to, also, become part of the Kiev battle. It was to be the end of September before the division was back in position again facing Moscow, this time part of Hoepner's Pz-Gr 4. **Reich** was the only one of the SS units to participate in "Typhoon", the assault on the Russian captial. Setting out from Roslavl toward Borodino against strong Russian resistance, losses were so high that by 14 October the Totenkopf regiment [**SS-Inf-Rgt. 11**] that had been added to replace **Germania** was broken up among the **Deutschland** and **Der Führer** regiments in an attempt to keep them up to strength. The division had reached Mozhaisk five days later, 49 miles from Moscow, when mud halted advances. A full month would pass before the final drive began, by now too late to be successful. The attack reached Lenino, within 20 miles of the Kremlin, when it ground to a halt on 2 December 1941 in the face of one of the worst Winters on record and massive Russian reinforcements. The drive was officially halted three days later.

The SS goes to war, sending its motorized grenadier regiments into action. In this unique view, taken during the invasion of Poland, two Kfz 15 Mercedes-Benz 230s of Leibstandarte paused on a Polish backroad. Considerable effort has been made to suppress the identity of these troops. The "SS" has been at least partially masked on both license plates, the troops have had their collar tabs removed and cuff titles covered over. [Scott Van Ness]

On 12 January 1942, **Reich** having just moved into Winter positions between Staritsa and Gzhatsk, the first Russian Winter counterattack struck. What followed was over a month of a kind of Winter battle for which the German forces were neither equipped nor trained. For one terrible 17 day period, **Der Fuhrer** regiment was assigned the task of closing the ring behind the trapped Russian 39th Army and stopping all attempts at a breakout. (In closing the gap, **DF** linked up with the **SS-Kavallerie-Brigade** which had been mopping up resistance behind the lines until caught by the Winter attacks.) By the time it was over, **Der Fuhrer** was down to 35 men, and 2nd company having been wiped out to a man.

Meanwhile, **Totenkopf** had been fighting its own war of attrition in the North. First seeing action on 6 July 1941 in the vicinity of Daugavpils, within weeks it was being used to seal off Russian penetrations, a duty the division was to see frequently in the next year. Initially Northwest of Lake Ilmen and then South of the lake, **Totenkopf** successfully repulsed a series of enemy counterattacks, by mid-August being placed in immediate reserve between Lakes Ilmen and Seliger. It was to remain in that position relatively uneventful until 12 January 1942, when the Russian Winter counteroffensive in the North was launched. After fighting against overwhelming odds alongside 2. Armee-Korps for three weeks, **Totenkopf** found itself encircled in the vicinity of Demyansk. The actual

A lineup of LAH armored cars is seen here on parade through Prague, Czechoslovakia on 5 October 1939. An eight wheel SdKfz 231 is being followed by a 232 radio car and a pair of four-wheeled 221s. The most noticeable change in appearance is the darkening of the center of the White crosses that had been carried into the Polish Campaign. The highly visible White crosses had proved to be excellent targets for enemy gunners and were quickly modified. [Scott Van Ness]

encirclement would last for slightly over two months, but the resulting salient projecting into the Russian lines at Demyansk was to be in existence for well over a year. **Totenkopf** however, was pulled back to the Lovat region and again placed in immediate reserve.

The lull that followed the successful containment of the first Russian counteroffensive brings to a close the first hectic period of Waffen-SS development. Starting this period with a strength of three loosely connected standarten, the Waffen SS had grown to a nominal complement of six divisions [**SS-Division "Nord"** being added in early 1941, never fully motorized] and a brigade, while a seventh division [**Freiwilligen-Gebirgs-Division,** later to become **Prinz Eugen**] was forming. Four of the divisions were motorized, but not one of them was at strength and **LAH** and **Reich** in particular had been decimated in the Winter fighting. The time had come for the units of the Waffen-SS to begin their next transformation.

6

The SS drives into France, mounted on Kfz 15 Mercedes-Benz 230 medium cars. Above can be seen a lineup of Leibstandarte 230s, each towing a trailer. To the left, a similar column of SS-V vehicles is halted in the center of a French town. The two lead cars are 230s, but the two visible to the right are Kfz 15 Horch medium cross-country cars each towing a 7.5 cm lIG 18 Infantry Gun. [Bundesarchiv]

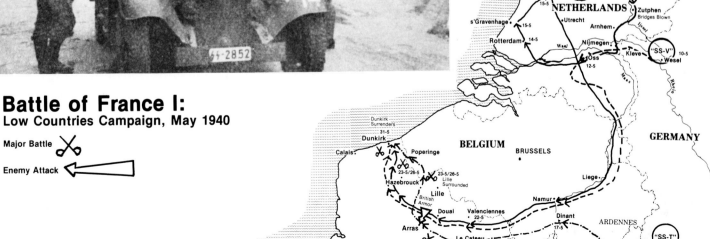

Battle of France I:
Low Countries Campaign, May 1940

Major Battle ✂

Enemy Attack ⬅

An interesting shot of Leibstandarte motorcyclists showing the beginnings of the unit's insignia. Barely visible on the front fender of the righthand BMW R75 is the key symbol that would become associated with LAH. The key was chosen in honor of the regiment's commander Josef "Sepp" Dietrich [dietrich is the German word for key]. The diversity in Leibstandarte markings during the French Campaign reflects in part some of the suppression seen during the Polish Campaign and in part the fact that these markings appear to have evolved from the bottom up rather than having been decreed by regimental command. Also the markings that were used varied considerably from the key alone to a key inside a narrow tilted shield as seen on some Pkws. [Scott Van Ness]

LAH
"Dietrich" [Key]

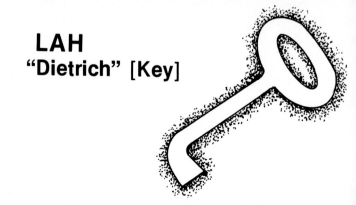

Three views of the motorized troops of SS-V in France. [Above] Four members of Headquarters SS-Standarte Deutschland are seen here riding in a Kfz 15 Mercedes-Benz 230 decorated with a swastika on the hood for air recognition. The soldiers are wearing transitional style uniforms. Three wear the costly, early Dark Green collared feldbluse, while the driver wears the later all Field Grey model. Note that none have collar insignia, as during this period the old style "SS1" collar tabs of Deutschland were being suppressed in favor of the universal "SS" pattern, though the lack of rank tab on the left collar is harder to explain. The regiment can still be identified, however, by the cufftitles visible on the nearer soldiers. [National Archives] [Center] Three troopers also from Deutschland [they still have the "SS1" collar tabs] wearily sitting in a 230 halted by the side of the road, pass the time reading. As opposed to the HQ troops above, these are combat soldiers and wear the camouflage smock over their feldbluse and cover for the helmet. [Bundesarchiv] [Below] The inevitable end result of mobile warfare, exhaustion overtakes two Sanis [Sanitäter = Corpsman] of the Pioneer Battalion.

Battle of France II:
Somme & Aisne Campaign, June 1940

Major Battle ✂

Note: "SS-T" used to mop up resistance behind the lines, movements not shown on map.

"LAH"......................................

"SS-V" —————————

An SdKfz 231 eight wheel armored car of Leibstandarte passes through a Southern French town toward the end of the campaign. At this stage there was great variation in the marking of LAH vehicles. The outline cross having been dropped, the only visible insignia on this particular vehicle is the tactical sign. [National Archives]

A column of vehicles of the regimental staff of SS-Standarte Deutschland is seen halted by a railroad crossing on the road to Libourne, near Bordeaux. Many SS-V vehicles carried a large white numeral next to the tactical sign indicating position in the unit. [National Archives]

The French Campaign completed, SS-V was earmarked for Operation "Sealion", the proposed invasion of England. Here a Kfz 15 Horch signals car practices disembarkation from a landing barge, bearing the same style markings carried during the just completed campaign.

Between the French and Balkans Campaigns, Leibstandarte became the first SS unit to acquire heavy armored vehicles with the addition of a Sturgeschütz Abteilung. Seen below and left are two StuG III ausf Bs of that unit showing some of the rapidly evolving markings displayed by LAH vehicles. The key without a shield appears here on the rear plate of the vehicle. Also on the rear of the vehicle are a dog's head symbol and a circle-dot insignia which is repeated on the front superstructure. A narrow White outline cross is seen on the side. [National Archives]

Two civilian pattern vehicles are seen here, pressed directly into service for Leibstandarte. [Above] A lineup of Chevrolet cars is seen halted by the side of a country road in France. The only concession to the military on these vehicles has been the painting out of the headlights. These vehicles carry another LAH marking, the White key in a faintly visible Black outline shield. There appears to be a tactical sign and small vehicle number on the opposite fender. [National Archives] [Right] A Ford G917T three ton truck is passing between two girls distributing the local military newspaper in Bulgaria, where LAH is preparing for the Balkans Campaign. Like the previous shot, the vehicle has the Black outline shield - White key divisional marking, above which is the vehicle number. [Bundesarchiv]

Balkans Campaign I:
Yugoslavia, April 1941

Two more views of SS vehicles moving into position prior to the Balkans Campaign. [Above] Reich, after going through considerable reorganization from SS-V, was sent to Rumania for final training before the invasion of Yugoslavia. Here a BMW R75 of the Auf-Abt passes in front of a line of curious Rumanian police. Of interest is the emergence of the divisional insignia, the so-called Kampfrune on the side of the sidecar. [Below] Displaying no visible marks besides the license plate, an SdKfz 220 four wheel armored car of LAH drives through Southern Bulgaria. The vehicles has been covered with a specially fitted tarpaulin cover and has had custommade "spaced armor" added onto the front. [Bundesarchiv]

One of Reich's original vehicles [as can be ascertained from the four-digit license number], a Kfz 15 Horch, is being passed by a column of Yugoslav prisoners during that division's brief participation in the Balkan Campaign. Of note is the small bundle of sticks tied to the front bumper in case mud is encountered.

[Above] Three recon vehicles of Leibstandarte are seen here on a road in Greece, being passed by civilians moving in the opposite direction. To the left is "Laforce", the same SdKfz 231 eight wheel armored car previously seen in Prague. Behind it is an SdKfz 232 radio car, and in the foreground an SdKfz 221 with the "field-fit" spaced armor. [National Archives] [Below] Seen at Patras, having crossed over to the Peloponnesus, a line up of LAH motorcycles passes a group of Greek civilians. These vehicles carry the vertical White shield and key marking that developed from the previous Black and White emblem.

Balkans Campaign II:
Greece, April 1941

Enemy Attacks
Major Battle

"LAH"
Florina
10-4
Vevi 12-4
Contact with Australians
13-4
Ptolemais
17-4
Kozani
Aliakmon
ALBANIA
Grevena
GREECE
Trikkala
Kardhitsa
Makrakomi
Mesolongion
24-4
Crossing by Small Boat
Patras
Tropaia
IONIAN SEA
British Surrender
28-4 Kalamata

Two shots of LAH armor during Barbarossa, the invasion of Russia. [Above] The StuG-Abt pauses outside Mariupol in Southern Russia. PzJg Is have been added to give the armored unit some anti-tank capability. Note that all three visible armored vehicles carry the same dog's head insignia of the StuG-Abt., first seen in France. [Right] Another shot from the same roll shows the next vehicle, displaying a nearly obscured outline cross, vehicle number and shield and key insignia. Note the shield now has the characteristic "cutout" in the upper right corner.

"Sepp" Dietrich, the legendary [and notorious] commander of Leibstandarte is seen here in full dress, carrying the rank of SS-Obergruppenführer, early in the Russian Campaign. [Bundesarchiv]

LAH

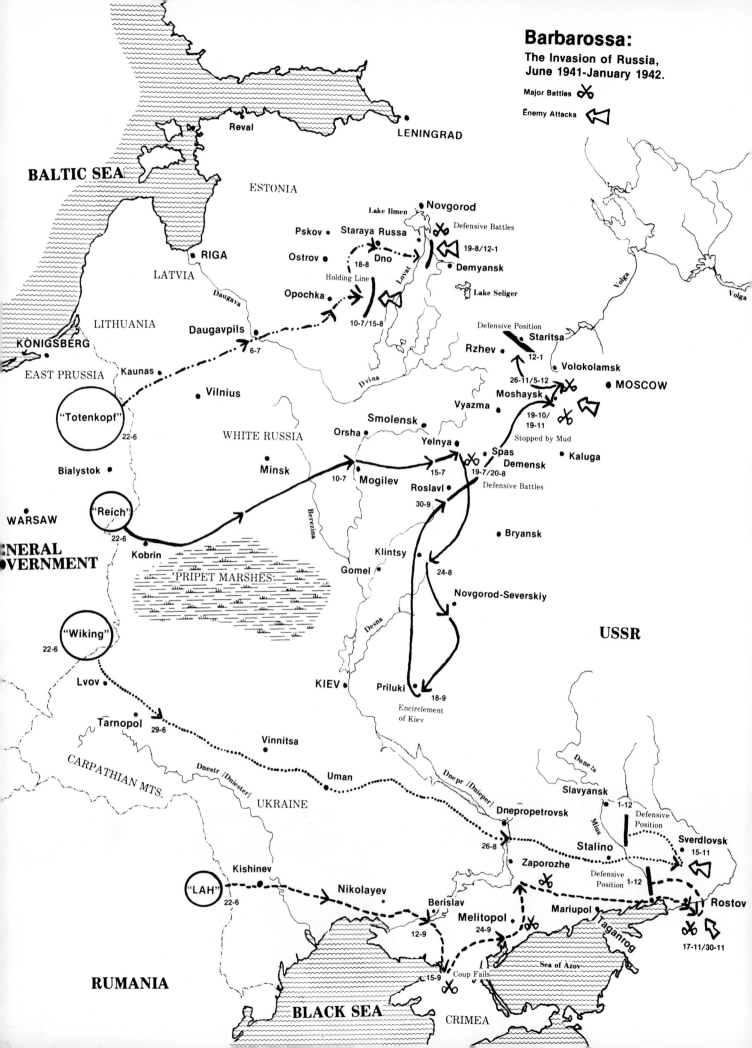

Barbarossa:
The Invasion of Russia,
June 1941–January 1942.

Major Battles ✂

Enemy Attacks ⟨

BALTIC SEA

Reval

LENINGRAD

ESTONIA

Lake Ilmen

Novgorod

Defensive Battles

Pskov · Staraya Russa

19-8/12-1

Ostrov · Dno

· Demyansk

18-8

RIGA

LATVIA

Holding Line

Lovat

Lake Seliger

Opochka

Daugava

10-7/15-8

Defensive Position

Staritsa

Daugavpils

Rzhev

12-1

LITHUANIA

6-7

Volokolamsk

KONIGSBERG

Dvina

26-11/5-12

EAST PRUSSIA

Kaunas

Moshaysk

✂ **MOSCOW**

"Totenkopf"

Vilnius

WHITE RUSSIA

Smolensk

Vyazma

19-10/
19-11

⟨

22-6

Orsha

Yelnya

Spas

Kaluga

Bialystok

Minsk

✂

Demensk

Stopped by Mud

10-7

Mogilev

15-7

19-7/20-8

WARSAW

"Reich"

Roslavl

Defensive Battles

22-6

Berezina

30-9

· Bryansk

NERAL
VERNMENT

Kobrin

Klintsy

PRIPET MARSHES

Gomel

24-8

"Wiking"

Desna

Novgorod-Severskiy

22-6

USSR

Lvov

KIEV

Priluki

Tarnopol

18-9

29-6

Encirclement
of Kiev

Vinnitsa

Dnestr (Dniester)

Uman

Donets

CARPATHIAN MTS.

UKRAINE

Dnepr (Dnieper)

Slavyansk

1-12

Defensive
Position

Dnepropetrovsk

26-8

Mius

Stalino

Sverdlovsk

15-11

Kishinev

Zaporozhe

Defensive
Position

1-12

⟨

"LAH"

Nikolayev

✂

Rostov

22-6

Berislav

Mariupol

Taganrog

Melitopol

✂

17-11/30-11

12-9

24-9

✂ ⟨

RUMANIA

C 15-9

Coup Fails

Sea of Azov

BLACK SEA

CRIMEA

Four views of Wiking, the new SS division, to be first blooded during Barbarossa. [Above] An SdKfz 232 eight wheel radio car carrying only a Yellow divisional marking, the so-called Sun-wheel, a variant on the swastika, is seen here against the background of the open spaces of Southern Russia. [Bundesarchiv] [Above Left] An SdKfz 221 four-wheeled armored car carries a couple of extra grenadiers as passengers as it heads into a Russian city. The tactical sign indicates that this vehicles belongs to Wiking's Auf-Abt. [Below Left] A BMW of Wiking is being pushed across a stream by its driver, passenger and a civilian helper. The letter "K" on the sidecar indicates Wiking's affiliation with von Kleist's Panzer-Gruppe in Southern Russia. Note the driver has a very non-regulation kerchief around his neck in an effort to keep out the all pervasive dust. [Bundesarchiv] [Below] Felix Steiner, the well respected commander of Wiking is seen in the foreground with an aide, poring over the seemingly endless maps of Russia.

Appearing almost identical to those seen during the Balkans campaign, this Reich BMW R75 motolcycle of the Auf-Abt Staff [St = Stab = Staff] halts briefly outside a burning Russian town.

Reich

An SdKfz 10 one ton halftrack of Reich is seen being followed by a Krupp Protz L2H143 gun tractor Kfz 69, more commonly known as Boxer. The White "G" indicates that Reich was part of Guderian's 2. Panzer-Gruppe. The use of a Wehrmacht vehicle, without bothering to change the license numbers, indicates the haste with which the establishments of the SS divisions had been increased between campaigns.

With Winter approaching, Reich found itself facing Moscow in Fall 1941. This well known shot deserves repetition because it shows a fairly rare vehicle interestingly marked and SS-Obergruppenführer Paul Hausser, the retired Army General who created the Waffen-SS and was conceded to be by far its ablest commander. The vehicle in which he is standing is an SdKfz 253 lGepBeokw observation halftrack.

Two shots of Totenkopf's war in North Russia. [Above] Two motorcycles take a brief respite from the dust of a Russian Summer, being passed by a truckful of troops. Of interest is the difference in the Death's Head marking between vehicles, a "common" shape not being found until the next year. Also note the red and white stop disc in the center of the lorry's tailgate, an early form of convoy spacing indicator. [National Archives] [Below] A Kfz 15 Adler 3Gd of Totenkopf's **Field Artillery Battalion** has managed to get itself mired in the sand. The trooper has not appeared to have had too much success in getting his car unstuck. He will probably have to wait for a hitch from a halftrack. [Bundesarchiv]

[Right] Not reaching divisional status for another year, the SS-Kavallerie Brigade was mainly employed behind the lines clearing up pockets of resistance. Though mainly horsed, the brigade did have mechanized elements. The tactical sign on the bow plate is too obscured to determine which part of the brigade this SdKfz 222 belongs. Inexplicably missing its 2 cm main armament, it has an MP 40 pushed through the driver's right front visor opening for added firepower. [Bundesarchiv]

Operation Typhoon, the drive on Moscow, was halted twice, first by mud and then by cold. The German Army was adequately prepared for neither. [Above] Two medium passenger cars of Reich are seen in the mud that could frequently mire cars axle-deep. On the left is a Kfz 15 Mercedes-Benz 230, to the right a Adler 3Gd Kubel. The divisional insignia is in Yellow, making it appear much fainter than the White G and convoy stripes. [National Archives] [Below] The first snow catches German formations without camouflage or cold weather gear. These Reich motorcyclists already look cold in their motoring coats and extreme weather was still several weeks off. The unexpectedly early Winter was equally hard on equipment and men, halting Reich within reach of the Kremlin. The lineup of PzKpfw IIIs probably are those of 10. Pz-Div., alongside of which Reich fought for most of Typhoon.

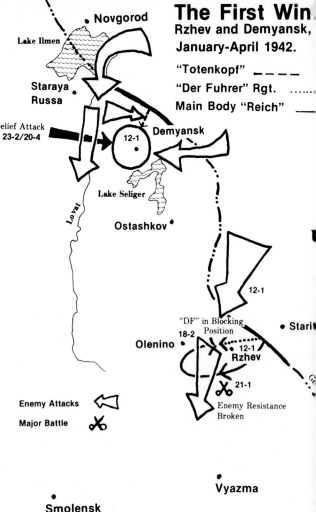

The First Win
Rzhev and Demyansk,
January-April 1942.

"Totenkopf" — — —
"Der Fuhrer" Rgt. ....
Main Body "Reich" ———

Novgorod

Lake Ilmen

Staraya Russa

Relief Attack
23-2/20-4

Demyansk

12-1

Lake Seliger

Ostashkov

Lovat

12-1

"DF" in Blocking Position
18-2

Olenino

12-1

Rzhev

Starit

21-1

Enemy Resistance Broken

Enemy Attacks

Major Battle

Vyazma

Smolensk

Having spent the Winter involved in the bloody fighting around Demyansk, Spring brought Totenkopf some much needed rest and a chance to prepare for a quieter Summer between Lake Seliger and Lake Ilmen. [Top] An SdKfz 9 Famo 18 ton halftrack is seen among the pines. [Bundesarchiv] [Center] In a rare idyllic moment on the Eastern Front. Three Totenkopf troopers, two wearing shorts, are washing the Spring mud and Winter camouflage off their trucks. [Bundesarchiv]

Immediately prior to being sent to France for a much needed refit, this SdKfz 250/11 ISPW light armored personnel carrier of LAH is seen in position in a South Russian cow pasture. The 250/11 was a recon company leader's vehicle mounting the squeezebore 2.8 cm schwere Panzerbüsche 41 light anti-tank gun. Note the rather casual attempt at natural camouflage by draping a few clumps of straw over the fenders of the vehicle. [National Archives]

A far cry from the Eastern Front, a lineup of three civilian style cars of Leibstandarte's war correspondant troop are halted by the side of the road while the occupants admire the scenery in sunny France. The wreath of leaves around the shield and key divisional insignia is in honor of the award of the oak leaves to the Knight's Cross to "Sepp" Dietrich. This style of unit marking was carried by LAH vehicles during its stay in France, Summer 1942. Each car also carries the KB [Kriegsberichter] insignia of the war correspondant. [Bundesarchiv]

Coming of Age: Summer 1942-Summer 1943

The Summer of 1942 saw the exhausted motorized formations of the SS pulled back individually for much needed refit and reinforcement. It was a process from which they were to emerge for the first time as full fledged armored units. Before the year was over, they were to be the key elements in the most spectacular counteroffensive launched by the Germans during the war.

The first of the SS units to be pulled out of line was the most badly mauled, **Reich**. The bulk of the division entrained for France at the beginning of March 1942, leaving behind most of its equipment and a battalion-sized formation [**Kampfgruppe Ostendorf**] to continue to back up the front near Rzhev. **Ostendorf** stayed in that general area until relieved in mid-June, whereupon it rejoined the bulk of the division, now at Bergen, Norway. The Totenkopf regiment that had been broken-up on the drive to Moscow was replaced by a new third regiment, **Langemarck**, this one fully motorized. As with the other three motorized SS divisions, **Reich** received a Panzer-Regiment to bring it up to Panzer-Grenadier division strength. It was also renamed twice again, in May becoming the more grammatical **SS-Division "Das Reich"** and in November, in acknowledgement of its new composition, **SS-Panzer-Grenadier-Division "Das Reich"**. It was to stay in training until recalled to the Eastern Front along with **LAH** and **Totenkopf** in late January 1943, in response to the crisis that threatened the German positions in Russia following Stalingrad.

Leibstandarte followed a similar course. It was withdrawn from its positions on the Mius in June 1942, being pulled back to France, where it was based just outside Paris. Re-equipping and refitting, **LAH** followed the pattern of **Das Reich** very closely, even down to being renamed. In September it became **SS-Panzer-Grenadier-Division "Leibstandarte SS Adolf Hitler"**. And as with its SS companions it remained in the West until recalled to Russia in January 1943.

In contrast, **Totenkopf** remained in its position behind the Lovat in North Russia until late October 1942. Only then was it withdrawn to France for what was to be a much shorter refit period. In November it was renamed **SS-Panzer-Grenadier-Division "Totenkopf"** taking part immediately in the occupation of Vichy France. **Totenkopf** remained in Southern France until recalled as part of the **SS-Panzer-Korps**.

Alone among the "original" SS divisions, **Wiking** was not withdrawn to France for refit, but was reinforced while in position on the Mius. There it received the same strengthening, including a Panzer-Regiment. And it was the first to test its new armor, as it assigned to the 57. Panzer-Korps along with 13. Panzer-Division and given a leading role in the upcoming Summer offensive. The drive was launched 19 July 1942, **Wiking** seeing heavy fighting from the start, first in the drive on Rostov and then on to the oil fields of the Caucasus. By September part of the oil fields was in German hands, but the attacks had ground to a halt, strangled by the very distances they had covered. At the same time that the division was renamed **SS-Panzer-Grenadier-Division "Wiking"** in November 1942, the attack was formally called off and defensive positions taken along the Terek. The Russian attacks at Stalingrad finally forced the Germans to acknowledge the weakness of their position in the Caucasus and heralded the retreat of Armee-Gruppe A from the South. By January 1943, when the other SS formations were arriving to help stem the crisis on the Donets, **Wiking** was back at the Manych, holding open the retreat route through Rostov. At the same time that the Manstein Offensive was clearing up Russian penetrations south of Kharkov, **Wiking** was similarly employed in mid-February containing the attack of the First Guards Army south of Izyum. When the last Russian resistance had been crushed in late February 1943, the division was in much the same position it had been in a year before, behind the Mius and in need of a refit.

At the same time that the Russians were tightening the noose around 6. Armee in Stalingrad, plans were being laid for the hoped for dismemberment of the entire German Southern Front by a series of armored attacks. The attacks were intended to split the German armies into easily manageable pieces and push them back against the Black Sea and the Dnieper. It is fortunate for the Germans that the Stalingrad crisis caused the recall of first two and then the third of the SS-Panzer-Grenadier-Divisions in France, giving an adequate armored force immediately available when crisis threatened on the Donets. And fortunate too for the obstinace and audacity of a former Army Generalleutnant without whom that reserve might have ceased to exist before its greatest battle.

Having been ordered from France in late January 1943, **LAH** and **Das Reich** arrived in Russia in early February and were immediately thrown into the defense of Kharkov. The adhoc **SS-Panzer-Korps**, under the command of SS-Obergrüppenfuhrer Paul Hausser, went into combat on 11 February with specific instructions from Hitler to hold the city at all costs. Within two days, Hausser was requesting to be released from this condition

as the city was being increasingly outflanked to either side. It was a request that fell on deaf ears, as Hitler insisted that "his" SS, above all others, should follow his orders to the letter and without question. Thus Hausser found himself caught between the order to hold the city and the obvious fact that within days the **SS-Panzer-Korps** and its magnificent mobile striking force would be encircled and forced into costly street fighting for which it was least suited. When, by the morning of 15 February, a single road only linked Kharkov to German lines, Hausser chose to save his divisions, ordering them out of the city, informing a furious Hitler only after the fact. It was these divisions, **LAH** and **Das Reich**, along with the newly arrived **Totenkopf**, that Manstein used to eradicate the penetrations of the Russian Third Tank Army. So obviously correct was Hausser's decision, that in spite of the fact that Hitler's immediate reaction had been to order him shot, Hausser was never officially reprimanded for his direct disobedience.

Not only were the three SS units able to help entrap the Russian spearhead, but they then led the most successful German counterattack of the war. Having cleared up the last enemy resistance south of Kharkov by 3 March, the **SS-Panzer-Korps** started a bold sweep around that city to envelop any remaining Russians west of the Donets. It must have been a source of great personal satisfaction for Hausser when on 11 March his troops were again fighting in the streets of Kharkov, this time as part of a victorious army sweeping the disorganized enemy before them. By 18 March 1943, the three SS Division had taken Belgorod, held a bridgehead across the Donets and stood poised behind the exposed flank of the entire Russian Central Front. Visions of Moscow again danced in German heads, and even the Russians begrudgingly admit that they were never closer to defeat. There were no more reserves available to the enemy, everything had been risked in the vain attempt to destroy Heeres-Gruppe Süd, and now nothing could stop the tanks of **SS-Panzer-Korps** from rolling up the flank of the enemy, except exhaustion, mud and Hitler.

The last of those foes was to prove the most disastrous. The mud of a Russian spring brings operations to a halt for three to four weeks. It would take five weeks, Manstein figured, to totally rest and refit his units. He was ready to move at the beginning of May. Manstein's offensive could have been resumed with a minimum of difficulty. The Russians had only been able to plug the holes in their front at Belgorod by weakening it elsewhere and throwing in poorly trained scratch formations. A breakthrough now, a very real possibility, would find the

While LAH and Reich **were refitting in France and** Totenkopf **spent a quiet Summer in North Russia,** Wiking **spearheaded the German drive into the Caucasus, again part of von Kleist's 1. Panzer-Armee. [Above]** Wiking **took its new Panzer Regiment into action immediately. Seen on the outskirts of Rostov are two PzKpfw IIIs, on the left an ausf J and on the right a PzBefWg III ausf H. The ausf J has the divisional insignia on its near fender. Both are in overall Panzer Grey. The lack of a main armament for the command tank makes camouflage more important, hence the amount of foliage carried. [Bundesarchiv] [Below] In the waist deep grass of the Kuban Steppes, a recon team with their nearly hidden SdKfz 222 scans the horizon.**

Russians even weaker than before on the rest of the Front and utterly lacking in reserves.

But Hitler said no. Tigers, Ferdinands and Panthers were beginning to appear or were promised and Hitler wanted his armies, particularly the SS, re-equipped with these new superweapons. Also, he claimed, he wanted to draw more Russian troops into the salient that now existed between Belgorod and Orel, so that when it was cut off, that alone would be disastrous to the Russians. Instead of an attack only from the South aimed eventually at Moscow, Hitler wanted to build up the forces at Orel as well, and launch a predictable pincer attack aimed only at pinching off the now strengthened Russian forces

A sight too frequently encountered in the drive for the Caucasian oilfields. As here at Maykop, which Wiking took on 1 August 1942, the retreating Russians would fire the fields, destroying pumps, wellheads and towers, making the oil useless to the enemy. [Bundesarchiv]

Drive to the South:
To the Cancasus and Back,
July 1942-January 1943

Major Battle ✂

"Wiking" ─────

Slavyansk
19-7
30-1
Stalino • Sverdlovsk
Mius
22-7
Taganrog
Mariupol • ROSTOV
26-7
USSR
Proletarskaya
12-1
Elista
Kerch
Kuban
Kropotkin 1-8
Krasnodar
Maykop 1-8 Armavir
13-8/20-9
Kuma
Tuapse
Holding Bridgehead
20-11/10-12
BLACK SEA
Grozn
25-9 25-10/1
Stoppe
Alagir Ordzhoniki
Sukhumi 13-11
Relieving
Encircled 13 PzD
Batumi

Taking notes on the enemy. Here three Wiking grenadiers check out an abandoned Russian T-34C. Moving past in the background is a Wespe [officially 1FH 18/2 auf Fgst PzKpfw II [Sf] SdKfz 124], a self-propelled 10.5cm howitzer on the PzKpfw II chassis. Completely bare of markings, the Wespe is painted overall Desert Brown, a Yellow-Brown color adapted for the DAK in Tunisia, but also used on vehicles in the Caucasus.

around Kursk. But to do this, to create a second equivalent striking force under Model at Orel would take time. It was time that Germany did not have.

It was time the Waffen-SS nevertheless used to advantage. The three divisions of the **SS-Panzer-Korps**, in particular, were tremendously reinforced, gaining a Tiger-Abteilung each. All four of the original SS motorized divisions were strengthened and brought to a peak of preparedness. Elsewhere the Waffen-SS had continued its growth. Four more divisions, all armored, and an assault brigade [**Sturmbrigade "Reichsfuhrer SS"**], were added to the eight already in existence [**SS-Kavallerie-Brigade** becoming **SS-Kavallerie-Division** in 1942]. The new divisions [**SS-Panzer-Grenadier-Division "Hohenstaufen"**, [10.] **SS-Panzer-Grenadier-Division "Karl der Grosse"**, [11.] **SS-Panzer-Grenadier-Freiwilligen-Division "Nordland"** and **SS-Panzer-Grenadier-Division "Hitlerjugend"**] were in various stages of assembly and training, none would be combat ready before the end of 1943.

Thus the Waffen-SS now had a nominal armored strength of eight divisions. But it was on the four "original" SS-Panzergrenadier divisions that all eyes were focused as Summer approached in South Russia, particularly the three of

SS-Panzer-Korps, LAH, Das Reich and **Totenkopf.** They represented the most Germany had to offer in both men and equipment. They were fine, strong and victorious. Much was expected of them. They would never again be as strong.

All good things must come to an end; the enemy offensive that surrounded Stalingrad and drove deep wedges into the German Front in Southern Russia required the recall of the three SS-Panzer-Grenadier-Divisions that had been refitting in France. LAH and Das Reich were thrown into the defense of Kharkov in early Winter 1942. Newly arrived from France, this PzBeoWg III ausf H observation tank of Leibstandarte is camouflaged with Dark Green stripes sprayed over the Panzer Grey base. Note the unusual "Luftwaffe" style cross on the superstructure side, having a Black center [which became common later on Sand Yellow vehicles] and a Black outline to the White Balkenkreuz. Note also the turret schurzen, designed to protect against hollow-charge weapons like the Russian magnetic mine. The uniforms of the crew show the magnificent standard of equipment of SS troops. The reversible parka that all three are wearing Mouse Grey side out was exclusively as SS item. [Scott Van Ness]

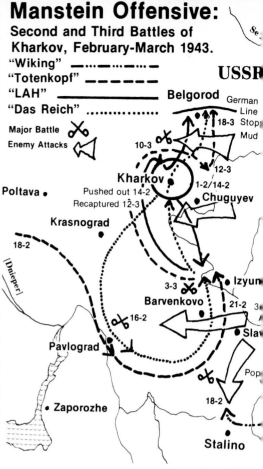

"Wiking" —··—··—··—
"Totenkopf" — — — — —
"LAH" ——————
"Das Reich" ················

Major Battle ✄
Enemy Attacks ⤲

USSR

Belgorod
German Line Stop Mud

18-3
10-3
12-3
Kharkov
1-2/14-2
Poltava
Pushed out 14-2
Recaptured 12-3
Chuguyev
Krasnograd
18-2
[Dnieper]
3-3
Izyun
Barvenkovo
21-2
16-2
Pavlograd
Sla
Pop
Zaporozhe
18-2
Stalino

Manstein rallied the German forces that were forced out of Kharkov. In a series of brilliant maneuvers, led by the SS-Panzer-Korps, the enemy thrusts into German positions were destroyed and Kharkov and Belgorod were taken back from the Russians. [Above] Two *Leibstandarte* vehicles are seen during the recapture of Kegichevka, a town near Kharkov, in early February 1943. A PzKpfw IV ausf G leading a Kfz 15 Horch is surrounded by grenadiers with thin White camouflage coats over their reversible parkas. The tank has been snow camouflaged while the Horch has not, indicating priorities in the use of short supply items, such as White paint. [Below] Another PzKpfw IV ausf G of *Leibstandarte*, this one from the seventh company of the Panzer regiment. Of interest is the repetition of the cross on the superstructure side, the White outline fading into the camouflage leaving only the Black center visible. Against the snow and a White building, the camouflage is reasonably effective. [Bundesarchiv]

[Left & Center] Advancing down the main street of a Russian town, a PzKpfw III ausf J followed by a PzKpfw II ausf F, both of Leibstandarte, keeps a wary eye out for remaining pockets of enemy resistance. On the rear of both vehicles the national and divisional insignias have been left visible through the camouflage. Note that the wreath with LAH's shield and key emblem has been reduced in extent. This was to be the "definitive" style. [Bundesarchiv]

Passing in front of a field artillery battery, this "Stummel" of Leibstandarte makes an excellent study of the futility of temporary snow camouflage, wearing off almost completely where the engine or gun heat would melt snow or where the dismounting of the crew would rub it off. The Stummel [officially an SdKfz 251/9 mounting the 7.5 cm L/24 Kwk], a brand new vehicle at this time, was extremely popular because it brought massive fire-power to individual panzergrenadier companies. In the background are a pair of 10.5 cm lFH/18 Field Howitzers and a single SdKfz 11 three ton halftrack support vehicle. [National Archives]

Two shots of similar vehicles during the Manstein Offensive showing the deterioration of the water soluble Winter camouflage. [Left] A PzBefWg III ausf K of *Totenkopf's* first Panzer-Abteilung's headquarters company shows a pristine new coat of White paint at the beginning of operations. There is an even coat of camouflage over the whole vehicle, covering even the national insignia, leaving only a part of the driver's plate and the turret side unpainted to expose the divisional sign and turret numbers. [Bundesarchiv] [Below] An identical command tank, this time from *Totenkopf's* second tank battalion and seen a month or so later. The White paint is now wearing off in many areas leaving the original Panzer Grey to show through. Note the additional track shoes added on to the glacis and driver's plates for extra protection. [Bundesarchiv]

Having left Kharkov with considerable official disfavor, the units of the SS-Panzer-Korps were understandably proud of their recapture of the city. *Leibstandarte*, being the first into the city, was quick to rename the city's central Red Square as "Platz der LAH". As the offensive moved North to Belgorod, many support services were left based in Kharkov. The above signs, as well as showing the new name for the main square, point to the Field Hospitals [Feldlazarett] of all three divisions and give particularly clear examples of their divisional markings.

[Above] Spring is coming to Central Russia, as these armored cars of Leibstandarte fight their way into Belgorod. An SdKfz 223 radio car is seen being led by a pair of SdKfz 222 four wheel armored cars. The snow has almost disappeared and the ground is getting soft enough for the first wheel ruts to appear. On the 223, mud appears to have been applied to the vehicle sides to cover what remains of the snow camouflage. Note the prominently displayed national flags on the rear decks, evidence of total German air superiority. [National Archives]

[Below] Mud! The Manstein Offensive mires to a halt, perched on the flank of the entire Russian Central Front. In this crowded shot a wide variety of Leibstandarte vehicles is displayed. Halted to the right is an SdKfz 10 one ton halftrack of one of the Panzergrenadier-Abteilungen. Passing it is an SdKfz 250/1 light APC of a motorized artillery battery and beyond that is a line up of very early StuG III ausf Gs [again indicating that SS units got new equipment first] from the division's assault gun battalion. Note that all troopers once again are wearing their reversible parkas Mouse Grey side out. The camouflage canvas draped over the one ton's hood is of Italian origin. It is up to the reader's imagination to figure out which of many ways that could have gotten there. [National Archives]

While the three divisions of the SS-Panzer-Korps, **assisted by Wiking, were making military history, other SS units were engaged in much less glamourous, or successful enterprises.** The SS-Freiwilligen-Division "Prinz Eugen" fought the entire war, from October 1942 on, in the grim anti-partisan battles of the Balkans. Much like the American experience in Vietnam, the Germans were at best able to occasionally disorganize and dislocate the enemy, never to defeat them. And again in striking similarity, the superior equipment, organization and training of Prinz Eugen was no advantage, and was in some ways of grave detriment. Never being considered a "Front Line" division, Prinze Eugen was supplied mainly with captured equipment. Being a mountain-trained unit, the Bergmütze [mountain cap] and climbing boots were standard issue. [Above] Supported by captured French Hotchkiss H35s and wearing captured Russian snow coats, the men of Prinz Eugen set off on their first, and typically unsuccessful, major operation of the war, Unternehmen Weiss, in January 1943. [National Archives] [Left] Spring has arrived and suprisingly well equipped trooper of Prinz Eugen poses in front of one of the division's Hotchkiss tanks. Of interest is the Bergmütze which was to be the pattern for the later standard Feldmütze, and the divisional insignia, the so-called "Odalrune", replacing the normal SS right collar tab. [National Archives]

Two views of *Prinz Eugen* vehicles, dating from Spring and early Summer 1943. Many of the division's original complement of vehicles carried a Yellow Odalrune in a circle insignia, though later replacements most frequently did not. [Above] A Kfz 16 Horch medium signals car, seen here moving cross-country through typically Balkan terrain, carried the divisional marking on its near fender. The pennant on the opposite side indicates that this is a regimental HQ vehicle. [National Archives] [Below] This SdKfz 232 eight wheel radio car of *Prinz Eugen* seen in June 1943, appears to be virtually free of marking, only a license plate and hull side cross being visible. This is typical of the appearance of this division's vehicles for the remainder of the war. [Scott Van Ness]

The pause that followed the completion of the Manstein Offensive allowed the repair of worn vehicles and the addition of new. [Left] A rare shot of a halftrack workshop, full of both Wehrmacht and SS vehicles in various stages of repair. From the left, the identifiable vehicles are a one ton, a three ton with Sand Yellow overspray with another one ton and an eight ton behind it, a one ton missing its hood in the center and a twelve ton to the right. Of interest is the difference in the pattern of the license plates on the twelve ton. [Bundesarchiv] [Above] This PzKpfw IV ausf F2 of Das Reich has also had its coat of Panzer Grey oversprayed with the newly authorized Sand Yellow. [Bundesarchiv]

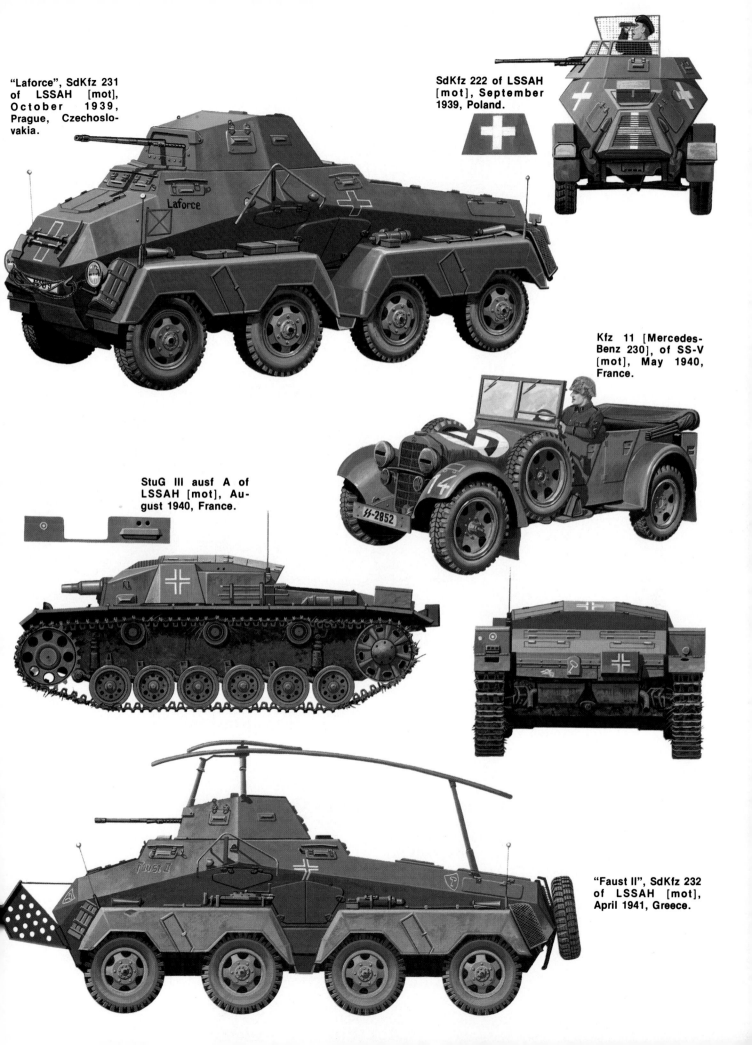

"Laforce", SdKfz 231 of LSSAH [mot], October 1939, Prague, Czechoslovakia.

SdKfz 222 of LSSAH [mot], September 1939, Poland.

Kfz 11 [Mercedes-Benz 230], of SS-V [mot], May 1940, France.

StuG III ausf A of LSSAH [mot], August 1940, France.

"Faust II", SdKfz 232 of LSSAH [mot], April 1941, Greece.

Two views of the new Tiger ausf Es that were being issued to the heavy tank battalions of the SS divisions. These Tigers of Das Reich are extremely early models, complete with the "S" mine projectors at the corners, early style cupola and Feifel air cleaning system. The tank to the right in the shot below is a PzKpfw III ausf M or N. Many new vehicles at this date were arriving still painted in overall Panzer Grey, these have had their original color oversprayed. In the view to the left, notice that in combination with natural shadow, this camouflage scheme was effective in breaking up the shape of the vehicle. [Bundesarchiv]

A rare vehicle, no more than twenty of these SdKfz 247/1 armored command cars were built, being issued solely to elite units such as the Wehrmacht's Grossdeutschland and LAH. The extremely low license plate number indicates that this was one of the division's original vehicles. [Bundesarchiv]

Decline: Summer 1943-Summer 1944

The attack that began on 5 July 1943 against the Kursk salient was code named "Zitadelle". The salient that just ten weeks before had been only weakly held now was jammed with enemy troops. 40% of Russian forces, and a full 90% of their armor was concentrated at or behind Kursk. On both fronts of the salient, the Germans had arrayed a force of 19 armored divisions. The attack was to be the greatest, and most wasteful, armored offensive launched by Germany. Very nearly successful, in the longrun was to prove a disaster from which the German armed forces were never to recover.

In the center of Manstein's formations on the southern edge was the **SS-Panzer-Korps** attacking just west of the Donets toward Oboyan and Kursk. Facing it was the Russian Sixth Guards Army including two complete Guards Tank Corps. Stalin was taking no chances. Yet when the attack came, the SS had success. The Russians were being beaten.

Led by their own Tigers and the Panthers of the hastily assembled Panther Brigade attached to **Das Reich**, holes were being punched in the Russian lines. Help came from the sky as well, as tank-busting Stukas paved the way for the SS tanks. So rapid was the advance that by noon on 6 July, the **Der Führer** regiment of **Das Reich** had taken Luchki I, 20 miles deep into the defenses. From there on resistance stiffened as SS-Panzer-Korps found itself taking on the crack Fifth Guards Tank Army pressing in from the east. 3. Panzer-Korps, East of the Donets, which was to have held this flank open for **Das Reich**, was disastrously slow in coming into action.

Nevertheless, by 11 July LAH and **Das Reich** had taken positions on either side of Prokhorovka, another 20 miles into Russian lines. At the same time **Totenkopf** had forced a crossing of the Psel on the flank of enemy defenses at Oboyan, poised to drive the remaining 40 miles to Kursk. There they sat for six days. Without their flank protected, **LAH** and **Das Reich** were forced to remain facing East rather than North, and without the support of the other two divisions, **Totenkopf** could not move. They were not to move forward from there. On 17 July, when 3.

Panzer-Korps had finally recrossed the Donets to fall on the flank of the 6th Guards Tank Army, Hitler lost his nerve. In response to desperate Russian attacks North and South of the salient, and the Allied landings on Sicily, "Zitadelle" was called off and the SS units ordered to Italy.

In actual fact only **Leibstandarte** was sent to Italy. Before **Das Reich** and **Totenkopf** could entrain, a more immediate crisis loomed on the Mius. They were promptly sent South to counter Russian penetrations toward Stalino. Their attacks were successful and by 3 August the Mius line was re-established. No sooner had that problem been solved than their services were once again required to the North. For the third time in a year, Hausser led **Das Reich** and **Totenkopf** into Kharkov on 12 August 1943. This time, however, the stay was brief. Hard pressed on both sides of the city, the two divisions soon found their positions untenable and on 22 August they were pulled out of the city for the last time. They then joined the now general retreat on the Dnieper, heading towards Kiev. By early September, **Das Reich** and **Totenkopf** were in reserve behind Kiev awaiting developments.

Wiking, because its refit after the rigors of the previous Summer's campaigns had been only partial, had been held in reserve during the fighting at Kursk. When Russian spearheads broke through in the Orel region, **Wiking** was immediately dispatched in an attempt to seal the penetrations. The division, however, simply did not have the strength to stem the enemy advance. As with the rest of the German forces in Southern Russia, **Wiking** retreated toward the Dnieper, crossing the river

The battle of Kursk opened with perhaps the greatest concentration of armor ever assembled for one operation. This line up of late PzKpfw IV ausf Gs of the 7th Company of Leibstandarte's **Panzer-Regiment** approaches a horizon already smoking from the opening barrages of the battle. These brand new vehicles are painted overall Sand Yellow with an overspray of Red Brown. From this point on, Sand Yellow was to be the standard base coat on all new vehicles and, as time permitted, old equipment was repainted. But, understandably, a great variety in color schemes was evident throughout this Summer. [Scott Van Ness]

Kfz 11 [Mercedes-Benz 230] of SS-Div "Reich", October 1941, Central Russia.

SdKfz 222 SS-Kav-Brig, August 1941, North Russia.

SdKfz 261 of SS-Pz-Gren-Div "LSSAH", September 1942, Paris, France.

"Lousbub", Panzer-jäger 38 [t] Marder III [SdKfz 138] of SS-Pz-Gren-Div "LSSAH", February 1943, Kharkov, Russia.

PzBefWg III ausf K of SS-Pz-Gren-Div "Totenkopf", March 1943, Central Russia.

SdKfz 247 of SS-Pz-Gren-Div "LSSAH", April 1943, Central Russia.

SdKfz 138/1 "Bison" of SS-Pz-Gren-Div "Das Reich", July 1943, Kursk, Russia.

Tiger I ausf E of SS-Pz-Gren-Div "Das Reich", July 1943, Kursk, Russia.

Two more views of Leibstandarte vehicles during the Kursk Offensive. [Above] The crew of one of 6th Company's Tigers mounts their vehicles prior to returning to the action. The Sand Yellow has been generally oversprayed with Red Brown, while on the superstructure side that second color has been brushed on directly. The flag, used for air recognition, is being flown from the radio antenna. [Scott Van Ness] [Below] A unique shot showing a quiet moment in the midst of battle. Two Russian prisoners, one wounded, are being interrogated by the commanders of one of LAH's panzergrenadier companies. The captain [Hauptsturmführer] is wearing the Black panzer uniform smoking a cigarette, while his assistant, a Scharführer, is bending over the two prisoners removing his glove. The Scharführer carries his rank insignia in the form of two Green stripes on the arm of his camouflage smock. The SdKfz 251 mSPW from which they have dismounted is Panzer Grey broadly oversprayed with Sand Yellow and liberally covered with foliage. The two other 251s visible on the left appear to be overall Sand Yellow. [Scott Van Ness]

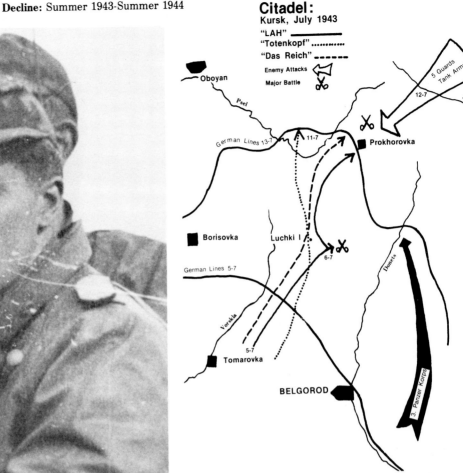

Jochen Peiper of LAH, later to become infamous in the West for his deeds during the Ardennes Offensive, gained his reputation for success and for ruthlessness in the battles at Kursk and after. He is wearing a motoring coat and an SS pattern camouflage cap. [Scott Van Ness]

at Gomel. It was then withdrawn to the Balkans for a complete refit.

After leaving its entire armored element behind in Russia to be split up among the remaining divisions, **Leibstandarte** spent its time in Italy training and once again re-equipping. As summer progressed, **LAH** received a complete new Panzer-Regiment including a Panther-Abteilung, and was at the same time renamed **1. SS-Panzer-Division "Leibstandarte SS Adolf Hitler"**. When the German forces in the East proved unable to hold the Russians and pulled back to the Dnieper, **LAH** was once again ordered back, this time to Kiev.

Unfortunately, Kiev would no longer be in German hands when **LAH** arrived. After taking positions behind the Dnieper in early November 1943, there had been a general redistribution of the SS formations. **Das Reich** remained near Kiev while **Totenkopf** was posted South to act in reserve behind the Dnieper front at Dnepropetrovsk. **Wiking,** upon its return from refit in December, was posted to the relatively quiet sector at Cherkassy. Meanwhile the first of the four new SS armored divisions, **Nordland,** came into action on the Leningrad front, where it was to see bitter fighting during that Winter's retreats to the Narva.

The end result of this dispersal of SS forces was that when the Russians broke through the Dnieper line north of Kiev in early November 1943, only **Das Reich** was in position to counterattack. And in a story that was to become all too familiar, it simply was not strong enough to stem the flood of enemy pouring to the South and West. In fact, by 6 November, it had

been forced out of Kiev to the Southwest. Only after desperate fighting were the Russian drives to the South blunted and finally halted at Fastov. But even with the arrival of **LAH** on 12 November, it proved impossible to throw the enemy back over the Dnieper.

This was not for lack of trying. Between 15 November and 30 December, **LAH** and to a lesser extent the much weakened **Das Reich** were involved in a series of counterstrokes, as part of Balck's 48. Panzer-Korps, that came close to achieving a major coup. First trapping three Russian Corps at Brusilov, then recapturing Radomyshl and finally attempting to encircle a large enemy force east of Korosten, **Leibstandarte** desperately tried to re-establish the German defensive lines around Kiev. In the fighting around Korosten the inadequacy of German strength again was shown. **LAH,** along with 1. and 7. Panzer-Divisions, threw a ring around seven Russian Corps. Not only could the encirclement not be held around so massive a force, but soon the Germans were fighting desperately to keep from being entrapped by their intended victims. By now the Russians had again broken through at Brusilov, overwhelming 24. Panzer-Korps, to which **Das Reich** had been attached. **LAH** linking up with the remnants of **Das Reich,** fought its way back through Zitomir, establishing a line in front of that city. Moved again, this time to Berdichev, **LAH** and 1. Panzer-Division halted Russian attacks there and by New Year won a well deserved month's rest. By now both sides were too exhausted to continue the fighting in the Ukraine, for a while at least. **Das Reich,** badly mauled in the fighting at Kiev and Brusilov, had

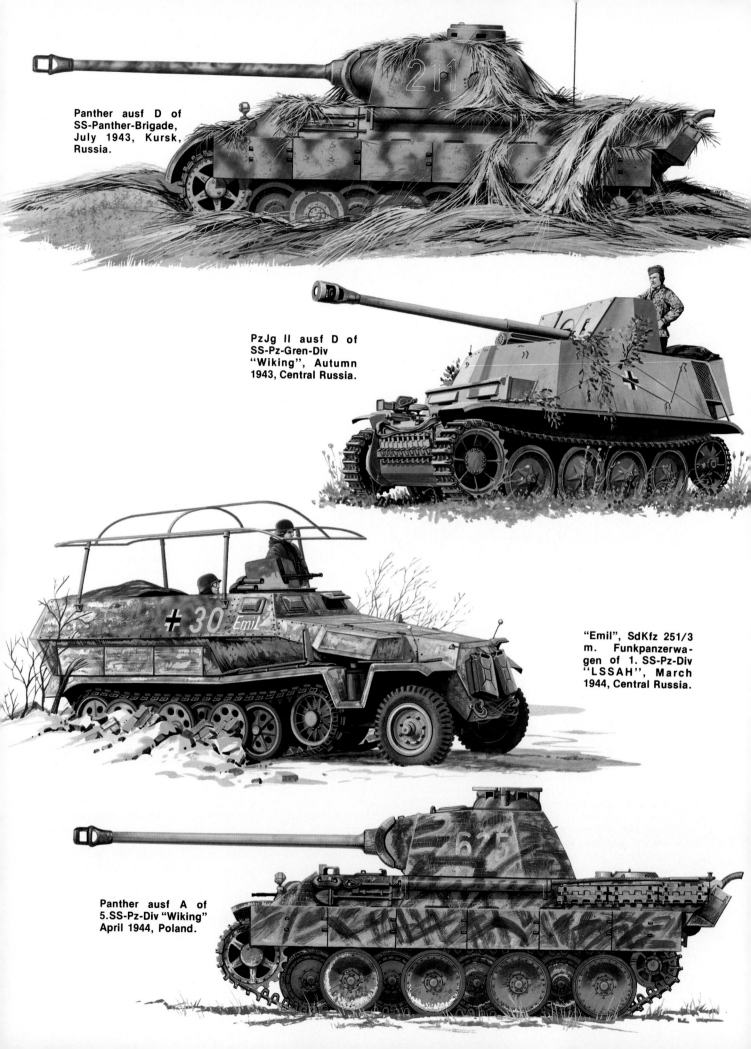

Panther ausf D of
SS-Panther-Brigade,
July 1943, Kursk,
Russia.

PzJg II ausf D of
SS-Pz-Gren-Div
"Wiking", Autumn
1943, Central Russia.

"Emil", SdKfz 251/3
m. Funkpanzerwa-
gen of 1. SS-Pz-Div
"LSSAH", March
1944, Central Russia.

Panther ausf A of
5.SS-Pz-Div "Wiking"
April 1944, Poland.

Panther ausf G of 1.SS-Pz-Div "LSSAH", May 1944, Paris, France.

Kfz 1 [VW Kubelwagen] of 12.SS-Pz-Div "Hitlerjugend", June 1944, Normandy, France.

SdKfz 251/1 of 5.SS-Pz-Div "Wiking", August 1944, Warsaw, Poland.

Panzer IV/70 of 12.SS-Pz-Div "Hitlerjugend", December 1944, Ardennes, Belgium.

SdKfz 250/1 of 11. SS-Freiwilligen-Pz-Gren-Div "Nordland", May 1945, Berlin, Germany.

[Above & Left] Two views of a convoy of armored vehicles of Das Reich on a dusty road behind the Kursk front. The 15cm sIG Bison seen above is Sand Yellow with a complex overspray of Olive Green. At the left is an SdKfz 251/1 mSPW carrying a member of the division's Feldgendarmerie [Military Police]. He can be seen leaning on the edge of the APC's fighting compartment, holding his Red and White traffic control paddle. [Bundesarchiv]

[Above Left] On their way to the front, a Kfz 1/20 VW type 166 Schwimmwagen and a Ford V-3000 three ton truck of Das Reich pass a Kfz 1 IPKW of the Luftwaffe. Both Das Reich vehicles carry the temporary divisional insignia adopted immediately before the Kursk Offensive to confuse enemy intelligence. The Schwimmwagen bears the markings of the division's Panzer-Regiment. [Bundesarchiv]

An interesting shot showing three mechanics working on the engine of a Das Reich SdKfz 231 eight wheel armored car. The spare tire obviously was missing before the vehicle was repainted Sand Yellow. Of interest is the plate upon which the divisional insignia has been painted. It was partly masked off during repainting, showing to good advantage the apparent difference in tone between Panzer Grey and Sand Yellow. [Bundesarchiv]

This Oberdsturmführer, probably a zug [troop] commander, sits perched confidently on his tank's cupola. He is wearing the rarely seen tanker's one-piece camouflage suit. [Scott Van Ness]

A mixed company of Das Reich tanks advances against the Russians. The two vehicles in the center background are late model PzKpfw IIIs, the rest being PzKpfw IV ausf Gs. All the Gs have turret schurzen, the nearest one is unusual in having side skirts as well. [Scott Van Ness]

the bulk of its forces pulled back to France in early February 1944. A regiment-sized battle group [**K-Gr Lamerding**] remained behind with **LAH** to continue the fight. The next round opened at Cherkassy. Having been halted to the North at Berdichev and to the South at Kirovograd (where **Totenkopf** had been engaged in bloody fighting alongside Grossdeutschland), the enemy came through the middle. Having been unable to encircle the German 8. and 1. Panzer-Armee, the Russians settled for the two corps that were still holding the Dnieper line between Kanev and Cherkassy. After some of the fiercest fighting yet seen, including a charge by three Russian Cavalry Divisions, the enemy broke through on 1 February to the North and South of the German salient, trapping six divisions, including **Wiking,** in a large pocket around Korsun.

The story of the previous year's fighting in the East had been one of just such encirclements and their attempted relief. Since the disaster at Stalingrad, the Germans had been successful each time in relieving surrounded troops and expected to be so again. On the basis of this expectation, the six divisions were told to hold their ground and await developments. But this was the largest such encirclement since Stalingrad and the Russians were determined that the same fate should befall these men as befell 6. Armee just a year before. The Germans brought up a relief force of four Panzer Divisions led by 1. Panzer-Division and **LAH.** It was to be strength against strength. Arriving in the area of Buzhanka on 3 February, **LAH** was launched immediately at the enemy-held neck of land separating the relief force from the encircled troops, specifically at the village of Shenderovka. In part because of gross miscalculation on the part of the German High Command (OKH), which caused the main attack to be misdirected for several days, and in part because four tired Panzer Divisions were simply not strong enough to break a line held in depth by two Tank and one Guards Tank Army, the attack failed. After twelve days of bitter Winter fighting the relief forces had penetrated no more than halfway through the 20 miles that separated them from the encircled divisions.

After only four days OKH had realized that, at best, any relief would require some assistance from the two trapped corps. On 7 February, **Wiking** was ordered from its position on the Eastern edge of the pocket to the Western, facing Shenderovka. On the evening of 11 November, the **Germania** regiment led the attack in the capture of that village. It then had to be held for five days against Russian counterattacks. When

Motorcyclist, SS-V Division, France, Spring 1940. He is wearing the Motorcyclist's Waterproof Coat.

SS-Mann, Assault Gunn Loader, Leibstandarte SS "Adolf Hitler" (mot), France, Summer 1940. He is wearing the Field Grey version of the Special Panzer Uniform. His shoulder straps are piped with the Pink waffenfarbe of armored troops.

SS-Sturmmann, Armored Car Gunner, Leibstandarte SS "Adolf Hitler" (mot), Greece, Spring 1941. He wears the Special Panzer Uniform. Note the Brown shirt and Black tie, characteristic of SS armored units early in the war.

Motorcycle Assault Trooper. SS-Totenkopf-Division, Russia, Summer 1941. He is dressed in a standard SS Camouflage Smock which has faded to the point that the pattern has almost disappeared.

Munitions Handler, SS-Panzer-Division "Totenkopf", Russia, Winter 1942. He wears the standard mid-war overcoat with felt and leather Snow Boots and fur cap.

VOLSTAD77

Panzergrenadier and SS-Ober-scharführer, Tank Commander, 7. SS-Freiwilligen-Gebirgs-Division ''Prinz Eugen'', Yugoslavia, Winter 1943. The grenadier is wearing a camouflage Shelter Quarter over a standard Mountain Uniform and Field Grey Toque. The Tank Commander wears the upper half of the standard Snowsuit under his Black Panzer Uniform.

SS-Unterscharführer, Panzergrenadier, SS-Panzer-Grenadier-Division ''Das Reich'', 4. SS-Panzer-Grenadier-Regiment ''Der Führer'', Russia, Spring 1943. Note the retention of the early style collar tabs and right shoulder strap in spite of being officially superceded in mid-1940. Otherwise he wears a standard Field Grey uniform and an SS-pattern camouflage cap. Note three of the many possible styles of medical chests.

Tanker, 5. SS-Panzer-Division ''Wiking'', Russia, Spring 1944. He wears the Reed Green denim Panzer Uniform with an Olive Green sweater. Note he carries a 1942 pattern gasoline can, the water can having different lettering. Note also the Army style cockade on his cap.

SS-Unterscharführer, Tanker, 1. SS-Panzer-Division ''Leibstandarte SS Adolf Hitler'', France, Spring 1944. He is wearing the late-war shortened Panzer Jacket and low boots. Note that SS tankers now wear a Grey shirt, similar to Army tank crew.

the realization finally dawned on OKH that **LAH** and the relief force were hopelessly bogged down still three miles from the pocket, permission was given for the encircled troops to attempt a breakout on the evening of 16 February. The breakout was to be led by a now much weakened **Wiking** division. After a day and a half of vicious combat the breakthrough was achieved, but at terrible cost. The divisions that linked up with **LAH** had suffered well over 30% casualties and the loss of nearly all heavy equipment. It was perhaps the greatest of ironies that at the same time that **Wiking** emerged from the Korsun Pocket completely denuded of fighting vehicles, it was officially reclassified as a Panzer-Division.

With the collapse of the front at Korsun, it became obvious to the German commaand that their lines had to be shortened. The Northern Front, which had been relatively quiet since the Spring of 1942, began to crumble during the winter of 1943-44. **Nordland** had been fighting there since November, in retreat since mid-January. Because of an almost total lack of tactical reserves in that area, OKH was forced to move some mobile units to the North. Anticipating a Russian drive on the Vistula, the nearly demolished **Wiking** and the relatively stronger **Totenkopf** were sent to Warsaw along with 19. Panzer-Korps. **LAH** along with **K-Gr. Lamerding** of **Das Reich** was pulled back to a new defensive line the Germans were trying to establish in the Western Ukraine.

It was a surprise to no one that the next Russian attacks in the South came as a pincer movement piercing the German front at Uman and Rovno. What was a surprise was when it came. A dry and early Spring limited the mud that would normally have halted all major operations for at least a month. Rather than April or May, the Russian Spring Offensive commenced on 4 March 1944, catching the Germans completely unprepared.

The German forward positions were overrun with little difficulty. Though **Leibstandarte**, part of 4. Panzer-Armee, began an immediate counterattack toward Rovno, it was not only unable to seal off the break caused by the attack of a Russian Tank Army, but was soon forced onto the defensive, retreating to the West. **K-Gr. Lamerding** of **Das Reich**, part of 1. Panzer-Armee, retreated Southward with the rest of that encircled army toward the Dniester and Kamentz-Podolsk. Within days the Russian wedges had driven over 50 miles deep into German-held territory, forcing the two Panzer Armies further apart. Manstein, commanding Armee-Gruppe Süd, was disturbed by the widening separation between his armies. If 1. Panzer-Armee continued to retreat to the South, it would be forced through the Carpathians into Rumania, cutting it off from the main front. And Manstein was unwilling to lose a force of 18 divisions, eight of which were armored. He ordered 1. Panzer-Armee to breakout to the West.

The task was to be formidable. A gap of 75 miles now existed between 1. and 4. Panzer-Armee, a gap held by four Russian armies. For the attack, slated for 29 March, the two armies were to push toward each other, hopefully to meet at Buchach on the Strypa. Two of the new SS divisions [9. **SS-Panzer-Division "Hohenstaufen"** & **10-SS-Panzer-Division "Frundsberg"**] were reluctantly allocated to the attack from the West. After seven days of hard fighting the linkup was effected, **Hohenstaufen** and **Frundsberg** [2.SS-Panzer-Korps] taking Buchach on 6 April. But as was the case in too many other such battles, the losses were appalling. The SS divisions, particularly **LAH**, were again in need of refitting.

Simultaneous with the encirclement of 1. Panzer-Armee in the South, the enemy also launched a minor pincer attack against German positions in Eastern Poland, surrounding Kovel. The subsequent relief attacks, involving first **Totenkopf** and **Wiking**, later on also **Hohenstaufen** and **Frundsberg**, were successful in re-establishing the link with the beleaguered city and holding the line which held until mid-July.

On paper, the Waffen SS was now a formidable force,

One of the vehicles that bore the brunt of the first attacks, a Tiger of Das Reich's **schwere Panzer-Abteilung [Heavy Tank Detachment].** During a lull in the action, some of the Tiger's accompanying panzergrenadiers dig in under the protection of the tank's big gun, within sight of a peaceful looking windmill. **[Bundesarchiv]**

comprising 17 divisions, 12 of which were at least nominally armored. In reality, it was not even close to this supposed strength. Of the armored divisions, none were at full complement. The most badly shot up were pulled back to the West to refit in anticipation of the Allied invasion. **Leibstandarte** and a reunited **Das Reich** joined the still forming **Hitlerjugend** and **Gotz von Berlichingen** in France. **RFSS**, having fought US troops at Anzio, was briefly back in the Balkans along with **Prinz Eugen**, while **Nordland, Florian Geyer, Hohenstaufen, Frundsberg, Totenkopf** and **Wiking** remained in the East. The Waffen SS was obviously no longer the small elite force that represented the Nazi racial ideal. The attrition of war and the manyfold expansion had long since diluted the ideologically-pure cadre that the Waffen-SS was to have been. The only attribute of its elite status it could still claim was that it was now, and until the end of the war, better equipped than equivalent army units. During this brief lull in the early Summer of 1944, the SS could still be considered a tremendously powerful force, if no longer the weapon it had been a year before.

**Das Reich
Kursk marking**

Das Reich Kursk marking

An interesting series of photos showing the Tigers of Das Reich in action. [Above] A captured Russian BA 64 light armored car follows a Tiger into the fight. This tank has already been through some action as can be seen from the damage to the Feifel system. [Bundesarchiv] [Left] Advancing across the rolling hills north of Belgorod, this grenadier leads a group of Tigers while more advance on the opposite ridge. The tanks of the Heavy Detachment were Sand Yellow oversprayed with Red Brown. [Bundesarchiv] [Below] An excellent closeup of the turret of "S13" [S = Schwere = Heavy]. The "Gnome" painted on the turret side was carried on most tanks of the sPz-Abt. [Bundesarchiv]

Mechanic and Tank Officer, 5. SS-Panzer-Division "Wiking", Poland, Summer, 1944. The mechanic wears the pants to the denim Panzer Uniform held up by suspenders, and a 1943 pattern Field Cap. The officer wears the Mouse Grey jersey shirt and belted camouflage pants.

SS-Panzergrenadier, 12. SS-Panzer-Division "Hitlerjugend", France, Autumn 1944. He is wearing a white shirt under his Field Blouse, visible at the rolled up cuffs, and the short boot with gaiters.

SS-Oberscharführer, Tank Commander, 12. SS-Panzer-Division "Hitlerjugend", France, Autumn 1944. He wears the commandeered U-boat leathers and a fur cap. He is holding an assembly flag, used for visual signaling to other tanks.

SS-Panzergrenadier, 12. SS-Panzer-Division "Hitlerjugend", Belgium, Winter 1944. He wears a rubberized rain cape over his camouflage smock and is carrying a captured pistol and cigarettes.

Volstad 77

Attached to Das Reich, though technically an independent formation, the Panther ausf Ds of the SS-Panther-Brigade are seen here in the three rare photographs. In the first shot two Panthers are seen dug into defensive position, extensively camouflaged with straw. The view below is of interest in that the vehicle numbers have been painted over the spare track links on the track side. These vehicles are in the regulation three color scheme, authorized in February but just coming into effect. [Bundesarchiv]

Advancing to the front, the lead vehicle of a company of PzKpfw IIIMs of Totenkopf are seen. The closest vehicle is painted in Sand Yellow with a rather crude Red Brown overspray. Note that the spare track links have been painted and oversprayed as well as the inside of the skirt armor. The vehicle immediately behind is an SdKfz 250/1 ISPW displaying the division's Kursk markings: three vertical bars above a horizontal cross bar. [Bundesarchiv]

Totenkopf
Kursk marking

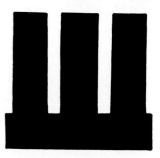

Two Tiger ausf Es of Totenkopf follow a StuG III loaded with grenadiers across the grasslands near Kursk. These tanks were to advance farther than any other German forces, pushing a bridgehead over the Psel. This photo illustrates well the limitations of any camouflage scheme. These vehicles are painted with the same colors and in a similar pattern to the those of Das Reich, but silhouetted against the sky and sun, they would still make excellent targets. [Scott Van Ness]

Three more shots showing similarities and differences between these Tigers of Totenkopf and those of the other divisions. Most striking is the relative lack of markings in comparison with those of Das Reich, here the divisional insignia was almost never seen on a combat vehicle. [Above] Hull-down near the top of a ridge, one of Totenkopf's Tigers is receiving an uncomfortably close return fire. [Bundesarchiv] [Left & Below] An interesting pair of shots of "111", before and during the action. Some days have passed between these photos. On the left it is seen moving into the fight in a line of similar vehicles, below it is halted during a pause in the activity to receive instructions. Note that the battle-damaged hull skirt was found to be a convenient place to store a jerry can. Note also the style of camouflage, composed of a random overlapping sprayed line of Red Brown over the base coat. The number was added later. [Bundesarchiv]

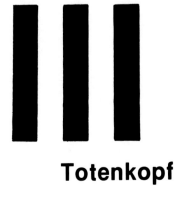

Totenkopf

Because of its exertions during the drive into and retreat from the Caucasus, Wiking was the weakest of the SS divisions at Kursk. For that reason it was held in reserve, seeing no action during the offensive itself, getting into the fight only during the following defensive struggles. It did however continue to receive equipment, always the newest and best. This is a fairly rare vehicle, an SdKfz 132 Marder II based on the experimental PzKpfw II ausf D. [Bundesarchiv]

An interesting shot of an SdKfz 9 Famo eighteen ton halftrack of Wiking's tank recovery company, seen hauling a captured Russian Valentine on a trailer. While the Germans did press captured Valentines into service in North Africa, it is unlikely that the same thing would be done here. [Scott Van Ness]

While the Kursk Offensive was called off largely in response to the Allied landings on Sicily, ostensibly because the elite SS-Panzer-Korps was needed there, in actual fact only LAH moved to Italy and saw no action while there. The main accomplishment was to pressure, by its presence, a skittish Italian government, and re-equip itself with new armor. Seen here on parade in the streets of Milan are a pair of brand new Sand Yellow, Red Brown and Olive Green PzKpfw IV ausf Hs. While the vehicles used by *Leibstandarte* at Kursk had been virtually unmarked, this more peaceful situation saw the re-emergence, possibly for the last time, of the shield, key and wreath emblem on LAH's tanks. [Scott Van Ness]

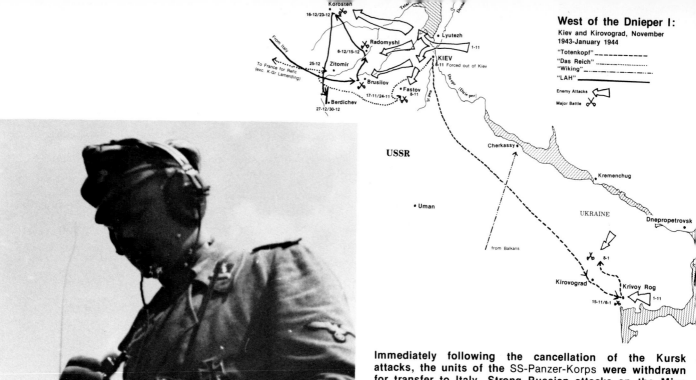

West of the Dnieper I:
Kiev and Kirovograd, November
1943-January 1944

"Totenkopf" ------------
"Das Reich" ------------
"Wiking" ------------
"LAH" ━━━━━━━

Enemy Attacks ⟵

Major Battle ⚔

Immediately following the cancellation of the Kursk attacks, the units of the SS-Panzer-Korps were withdrawn for transfer to Italy. Strong Russian attacks on the Mius positions west of Rostov forced an alternation of these plans and the switching of Das Reich and Totenkopf to the region of Stalino. These views of Totenkopf's StuG-Abt date from that period. [Left] An Obersturmführer adjusts his earphone volume while standing in the cupola of his StuG III ausf G. He is wearing the standard Field Gray assault gunners uniform. [National Archives] [Below] The men of a mortar platoon march across the rear of an advancing company of StuG III ausf Gs. Of interest is the three stripes insignia on the rear plate of the rear assault gun, this was a modification of the Kursk insignia adopted by Totenkopf in the Spring. [National Archives]

[Above Left] Another version of the three-stripe marking, this time in Black, can be seen of this early Tiger of Totenkopf. The four tankers visible are all wearing the one-piece tankers coverall and a variety of headgear. The solider straddling the barrel of the 8.8 is probably a grenadier just hitching a ride. Note the death's head collar tab, characteristic of the division's uniforms. [National Archives]

[Above] This Totenkopf Unterscharführer is an excellent study of a forward observer. Around his neck is the camouflage mask which would be raised up over his face. Presumably his Knight's Cross and collar insignia would be tucked into his smock in order to camouflage his entire upper body. [National Archives]

[Left] A well known shot, showing two grenadiers standing by the second company pennant of one of Totenkopf's motorized infantry battalions. These pennants were used as rallying points during combat, indicating the location of the company HQ. The three stripes may indicate the battalion number, or may be the divisional insignia.

[Below] A recon squad of Totenkopf's Auf-Abt mounts their SdKfz 250/1. The divisional insignia is faintly visible on the vehicle's front plate. The Fall mud has arrived and the Winter parkas have again made their appearance. Note the variety of fur with which the parka's hoods are lined. In the background is a StuG III ausf G. [National Archives]

The Winter's battles west of the Dnieper brought Leibstandarte back from sunny Italy to the snows of Central Russia. This snow camouflaged early StuG III ausf G is interesting in that its kills are denoted not only by rings around the gun barrel, a fairly common practice, but also by vehicle silhouettes on the superstructure. [Bundesarchiv]

A 7.5cm Pak 40 of LAH is seen here behind a natural camouflage of snow blocks. Note that while the front of the gun is painted White, everything behind the shield, and therefore theoretically invisible to the enemy, is still Panzer Grey. [Bundesarchiv]

An old friend, "S13" of Das Reich's sPz-Abt follows "S33" through the first snow of the Winter 1943. Last seen in the wheat fields around Kursk, these Tigers are now a little worse for the wear. Note the extensive damage to the external fittings such as the Feifel system, "S" mine projectors and hull skirts. In spite of the onset of Winter, these vehicles are still in their Sand Yellow and Red Brown camouflage. [Bundesarchiv]

Two more views of Das Reich **moving** through the woods near Berdichev. To the left above is a front view of two Tigers, to the right three PzKpfw IV ausf Hs follow a pair of Panthers. The PzKpfw IVs have a very even coat of Zimmerit on their turret schurzen. The nearest tank is painted overall Sand Yellow, the cross at the rear of the turret having been painted over sometime after the original paint job. The "Kursk-style" divisional insignia is still being carried. [Bundesarchiv]

While the Winter was just settling in around Kiev, the snow was deep where Nordland was engaged in North Russia. To the right are two views of that division's armor in the defensive battles back from Oranienbaum to the Narva. In the photo above, a line up of Tigers of SS-Pz-Abt 502, **attached to** Nordland's Pz-Rgt "Hermann von Salza". **Below** a close up of a StuG III ausf G. None of the vehicles display any recognizable markings, snow camouflage covering all upper surfaces.

The Winter of 1943-44 saw a continuation of the fierce fighting. For Wiking and LAH it meant the bloody battle of the Korsun Pocket, called Cherkassy by the Germans. Wiking was on the inside, Leibstandarte part of the unsuccessful relief force. This shot shows in excellent fashion how the men of Wiking appeared upon fighting themselves free. No longer adequately equipped, undermanned and totally without armor, the division was fit only to be withdrawn and entirely rebuilt.

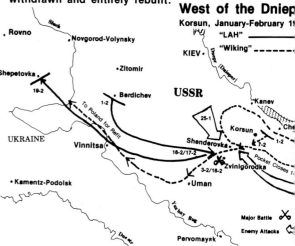

Part of the unsuccessful relief force, these two SdKfz 251 mSPWs of LAH are seen at Shepetovka during the brief lull in fighting, March 1944. "Emil", in the foreground, is a 251/3 radio halftrack while the 251/1 in the background is a standard APC. With Spring on its way in South Russia, the White paste camouflage is being allowed to wear off naturally. Note that while most visible troopers are wearing their parkas Mouse Grey side out, one grenadier still shows the White side. There was no specific date upon which whole units altered camouflage. [Bundesarchiv]

PRIPET MARSHES

German Pocket
Kovel

to France

UKRAINE

Rovno

Zitomir

Lemburg
[Lvov]

Holding Front

Berdichev

to France

Tarnopol Khmelnitskiy

Formed "Hedgehogs"

Relief Force
from France

Buchach

Vinnitsa

Bar

Dunayevsty

Kamentz-Podolsk

to France

Mogilev-Podolsk

Cernauti

Yampol

CARPATHIAN MTS.

Dnestr [Dniester]

RUMANIA

Major Battle ✂
Enemy Attacks

"LAH" _____
"Wiking" ....
2.SS-Pz-Korps _____
["Hohenstaufen" & "Frundsberg"]

K-Gr. Lamerding _ _ _ _
[Part of "Das Reich"]

The Russian Spring offensive caught the Germans unprepared, eventually surrounding the entire 1.Panzer-Armee in a huge pocket around Kamentz-Podolsk. The only SS unit caught inside was K-Gr Lamerding of Das Reich. but LAH and later Hohenstaufen and Frundsberg (2.SS-Panzer-Korps) were involved outside. These two views of Leibstandarte halftracks give some idea of what has happened to the magnificent divisions of a year before. [Above] An SdKfz 250/7 ISPW is seen here being followed by an SdKfz 223 four wheel radio car, through the ruins of a South Russian town. The halftrack is unusual in that it is in overall Panzer Grey, indicating that it was probably forwarded from a depot or training unit during the Winter under a coat of washable White camouflage, which has since worn and been rained off. There simply has not been time to repaint it the standard Sand Yellow. [Bundesarchiv] [Below] A lineup of SdKfz 251s move once again back into the fight. Led by a 251/9 "Stummel" support vehicle, the rest appear to be standard 251/1 ausf Ds. All are in a Sand Yellow base coat with a scruffy covering of Red Brown or dirt or both over it. [National Archives]

Two views of the vehicles of a rarely photographed unit, 16.SS-Panzer-Grenadier-Divsion "Reichsführer-SS" (RFSS), named after Himmler, which fought most of the war in Italy. [Left] Much of RFSS's equipment, as might be expected to a unit formed this late in the war in the territory of a wavering ally, was "liberated" Italian. Here two troopers ride an AS 37 scout car still in its Italian Yellow and Green camouflage. [Bundesarchiv] [Above] The armored element of RFSS was its StuG-Abt. A StuG III ausf G of the battalion is seen here dockside in a coastal city, probably during transport to the Anzio area where it faced the US landings, early 1944. The Black SS runes, also on the AS 37, are the only discernable unit marking. The national insignia is curious, having an extra Black outline. [Bundesarchiv]

Having wasted its strength in a year of desperate defensive struggles at the Mius, at Krivoy Rog and Kirovograd, Totenkopf was withdrawn to Poland to the Kovel region, to join Wiking and to refit. This photo, taken after the completion of the Kovel battle in April 1944, shows the vehicles with which it was fought, Panther ausf As and horse-drawn carts. The tank in the foreground is finished in the three-color scheme, and extremely rare for Totenkopf vehicles at this stage of the war, the divisional insignia on the glacis plate. [Bundesarchiv]

Upon its escape from Korsun, Wiking was sent to the Kovel region in Poland. There it was re-equipped one more time with at least eight companies of Panther ausf As. Each of these companies adopted a distinctive pattern of two or three color camouflage. [Above] "411" of the fourth company is primarily Red Brown in color, with Olive Green and Sand Yellow stripes. [Left] "231" is mainly Sand Yellow with broad bands of the other two colors. The vehicle is covered with a rough coat of Zimmerit anti-magnetic paste. [Bundesarchiv] [Below] "522", a fifth company Panther, has a light even spray of Red Brown mottling over the Sand Yellow base.

The Russian probes at Kovel in March 1943 brought Wiking back into the battle again. [Above] Another of Wiking's Panthers is seen in a probably posed, but believable, battle shot. The tank, number "635", is overall Sand Yellow with broad brush strokes of Red Brown and Olive Green. If this is an actual combat photo, the grenadier is a little close to the Panther for comfort. [Bundesarchiv] [Left] The panzer-grenadiers of 12.Kompanie Germania regiment pause by a burning building in Kovel. The SdKfz 251/1 in the background is numbered in Red with White outline. The grenadiers in the left foreground are in shirt-sleeve order.

Wiking

Some well known shots that deserve repetition because they depict a well known unit. SS-sPz-Abt 501. This was a unit formed around a cadre of tank aces from Leibstandarte. It was a corps-level heavy tank detachment attached to 1.SS-Panzer-Korps. The crossed keys emblem denotes its derivation from LAH. [Left] Michel Wittman, the most famous of the aces, is seen here, in the Black uniform, along with his four crewmen. The tanks and crews of sPz-Abt 501, and Wittmann in particular, were prime targets for photographers. That may explain the brand new appearance of all the uniforms. [Above] A Tiger of sPz-Abt 501 tows another that broke down during a training exercise. The lead vehicle is an extremely late Tiger ausf E. Note the all-steel road wheels. [Bundesarchiv] [Below] An SdKfz 1/20 VW Schwimmwagen follows a Sand Yellow and Green Tiger of sPz-Abt 501 past the church of a French town. [Bundesarchiv]

Two views of the interesting uniforms worn by crewmen of Hitlerjugend (HJ) tanks. The ability of German industry to produce the camouflage clothing required by the Waffen-SS, at a time when it was more than doubling in size, was far eclipsed by demand. This led, in the case of the divisions refitting or forming in the West, to the frequent acquisition of non-standard items of dress. The Italians proved to be a particularly useful source. [Above] An excellent shot of the commander of an HJ Panther. His tanker's tunic has been manufactured to German specifications from Italian camouflage cloth. [Bundesarchiv] [Left] Atop his late-model PzKpfw IV, this HJ tanker wears a uniform with a particularly convoluted history. It is a complete set of German U-boat leathers. Apparently they had been made for the Italian Navy but went into storage when it surrendered. Due to bureaucratic mix-ups, they never reverted back to the Kriegsmarine, and rather than let them go to waste, they were commandeered by Hitlerjugend. Nevertheless, one has to wonder about their practicality as a tanker's outfit. [Bundesarchiv]

Allied air superiority played havoc with German transport in the West. On this page are three examples of the extensive use of natural camouflage on vehicles both at rest and in transit. There can be no definite unit identification of the vehicles, though the one to left has been associated with Hohenstaufen around Arnhem, and the other two with HJ during the Normandy campaign. The vehicles are: [Above] an SdKfz 11 three ton halftrack, draped in net which holds considerable foliage, [Left] a late-model PzKpfw IV cover with branches and parked in some bushes and [Below] a column of heavily camouflaged StuG III ausf Gs, being passed by a civilian-style passenger car, under the protection of tall trees. [Bundesarchiv]

A rare opportunity to see four views of the same vehicle and its crew, in this case a Panther ausf G of LAH in Paris, immediately prior to the invasion. The shots above and below show the vehicle passing the Arc de Triomphe and parked in front of a lottery sign. Of interest is the camouflage, which is patches of Red Brown surrounded by Green on a Sand Yellow base, and the total lack of markings except for national cross. The views to the right show three of the crew, one in the Black Panzer uniform, one with the standard camouflage panzer coveralls over Black shirt and pants and one in a new looking two piece tanker's suit made from Italian camouflage cloth. Note that all wear the low shoes without gaiters. [Bundesarchiv]

Disaster:
Summer 1944 - Spring 1945

June brought the quiet late Spring of 1944 to an end. The battles were beginning that would lead inevitably to Germany's collapse. 6 June saw the Allied Landings at Normandy, 22 June the launching of the long-awaited Russian attack on Armee-Gruppe Mitte. From then until the end, the units of the Waffen-SS would be nearly continuously engaged. Refits would henceforth be infrequent, and inadequate. Inevitably the ability of even the SS to halt, much less drive back, the enemies crowding ever closer, began to dwindle. Toward the end, in spite of new divisions being authorized wholesale (up to a total of 38 or 45, depending on the reckoning used), the total power of the Waffen-SS continued to wane. There simply was not enough manpower or equipment to bring the "original" divisions up to strength, much less any of the newer ones. Despite continuing the struggle up to the final days, the divisions of the SS were powerless to do more than watch the final collapse of their world.

The Normandy invasion found the four SS divisions in the West widely separated. **LAH** was in Belgium, near Enghien as immediate reserve in the Pas de Calais area; Hitlerjugend [**HJ**] was near Dreux, due west of Paris, closest to Normandy; **Gotz von Berlichingen (GvB)** was at Thouars, south of the Loire; and **Das Reich** was at Cahors, in the Bordeaux region, nearly at the Spanish border. The German reaction was to the invasion immediate. **HJ,** being the closest, was ordered to make a rapid counterattack, aimed at driving the invaders back into the sea. The afternoon of D-Day and the next morning "Panzer" Meyer's tanks and grenadiers had some local success against the Canadians, but lack of experience and lack of co-operation with the neighboring 21.Panzer-Division (and in the opinion of some, lack of ability on Meyer's part) precluded any permanent gains. This was the beginning of a near-stalemate that was to last almost two months. For that time, the Germans, and the bocage country, limited the Allies to minimal and extremely costly gains.

One by one the SS divisions were engaged. Within days both **Das Reich** and **GvB** were in line against the US forces at the Western edge of the beachhead, between Coutance and St. Lo. And six days after the invasion, realizing that the forces available were insufficient, the German command ordered **Hohenstaufen** and **Frundsberg** from the Kovel area in Poland to the West at top speed. By 29 June both divisions were in line, in conjunction with **HJ** on the Odon. On 11 July, **LAH** was finally released from reserve, entering the battle on the Falaise road south of Caen.

The battles around the Normandy beachhead continued fiercely, and relatively successfully from the German point of view, for nearly two months. On the Western edge, **Das Reich** and **GvB** had held US forces to virtually no gain. In the East around Caen, where the Allies made their big pushes, the other four divisions had given some ground, but in general contained the attacks. On 12 and 26 June and 18 July the British and Canadians launched major offensives aimed at breaking through to the interior. In each case, the attacks were held. On 25 July the Americans had their turn, with different results. After a massive air and artillery bombardment, US infantry divisions broke through at St. Lo, opening the way for Patton's tanks. **Das Reich** and **GvB** were both roughly handled in the attacks, pushed aside and temporarily encircled at Coutance. In a fierce battle lasting 2 days, the two divisions cut across the lines of the American breakthrough, and while they were not nearly strong enough to seal off the breach, they were at least able to save most of their men and equipment, linking up with German lines at Mortain.

But the problems for the Germans in France were just beginning. The German Command, from Hitler on down, now began a series of incredibly bad moves that markedly worsened an already threatening situation. With Patton circling behind and the British still pushing in front, the Germans were being forced into an extremely vulnerable, narrow pocket between Falaise and Mortain. Two fairly obvious solutions presented themselves, either withdrawal from the pocket or attacking out of it toward Avranches, aimed at cutting off Patton. The Germans did neither for ten days. When an attack on Avranches was approved, it was too late and insufficiently strong. At the same time the position at Mortain was growing daily more untenable, the order was given to advance. **Leibstandarte,** which had been ordered first one direction then another for the last week, joined up with **Das Reich, GvB** and the Army's 2. and 116. Panzer-Divisions on 6 August 1944 for the attack (Unternehmen "Luttich"). The Americans, expecting just such a maneuver, held the Germans to virtually no gain. (The fact that 1.SS-Panzer-Korps, **LAH** and **HJ,** could field a total of 35 tanks while the US 2nd Armored, which was only one of the divisions facing "Luttich", had 250 must also be considered a factor.)

The attack, having been held, left the Germans in a worse

A frequently mis-identified photograph, this shows a Kfz 1/20 VW Schwimm-wagen of SS-sPz-Abt 501 driving down a road on which there is a PzKpfw IV of Panzer-Lehr on the left and a knocked out British Cromwell on the right.

Two views of Kfz 1 VW Kubelwagens of Hitlerjugend. [Above] The Kubelwagen is seen here following a line of HJ vehicles on the way to the front. Leading is a Panther, followed by an SdKfz 250/1 ISPW and two motorcycles. Of interest is the divisional insignia on the VW's right rear fender and the convoy marking, instructing the following driver to stay back 100 meters. [National Archives] [Right] A group of unhappy HJ troopers observe the craftmanship of Allied "Jabo" pilots. The Kubelwagen, which is Sand Yellow with Olive Green overspray and considerable mud, still has the shipping stencil visible on its door. Note the wide variety of uniform worn by the troopers. [Bundesarchiv]

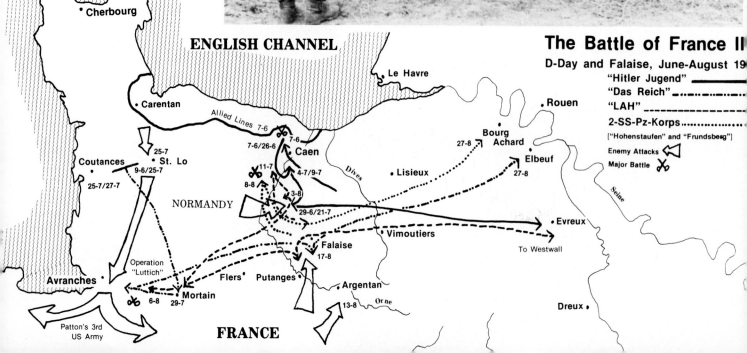

ENGLISH CHANNEL

The Battle of France II

D-Day and Falaise, June-August 19

"Hitler Jugend" ————
"Das Reich" —·—·—·—
"LAH" — — — — — —
2-SS-Pz-Korps ················
["Hohenstaufen" and "Frundsberg"]
Enemy Attacks ⊲
Major Battle ✂

• Cherbourg

Le Havre

• Rouen

• Carentan

Allied Lines 7-6

7-6/26-6   7-6

Bourg
Achard   27-8

25-7   St. Lo

Caen

• Elbeuf

Coutances •

9-6/25-7   11-7

4-7/9-7

Dives

• Lisieux

27-8

25-7/27-7

8-8

NORMANDY   3-8

29-6/21-7

Seine

• Evreux

Vimoutiers

To Westwall

Falaise
17-8

Operation
"Luttich"

Flers' Putanges •

• Argentan

Avranches •

✂ 6-8 29-7 Mortain

13-8   Orne

Dreux •

Patton's 3rd
US Army

FRANCE

position than had it never been launched, with three of their strongest divisions to the West of Mortain. They could do little more than watch Patton and the British attempt to close the trap on them at Falaise-Argentan, 30 miles to the East. In all, 19 German Divisions were nearly encircled. At this point, the only remaining question was how many, if any, of those divisions would be able to escape the trap. What followed was a race against time. The Germans began pulling some divisions out immediately (**GvB** being pulled out on 15 August) using others to attempt to keep the doors of the trap open for those still in the pocket. **LAH** and **Frundsberg** were pulled out soon thereafter, the first towards the Siegfried Line in the Saar, the other toward Compiegne. **HJ, Das Reich** and **Hohenstaufen** remained in the Falaise area at the North edge of the pocket. In spite of their best efforts, Falaise fell on 17 August. By the next day, the trap was closed behind the last of the German forces. The escape had been made, but again at a terrible cost in equipment. The remaining divisions, weakened by three months of fighting, fought unsuccessful rearguard actions across France. The Allied drive across Europe came to a halt at the end of August more from a lack of gasoline than stiffening German resistance. By the end of August, only **HJ** was still in combat attempting to hold up the Americans between Amiens and the Belgian border. The divisions of the Waffen-SS that had been engaged in the West were in appalling condition. **Das Reich** was down to 15 tanks, **HJ** to ten and **LAH** had none at all.

In the east, 4.SS-Panzer-Korps had been in action, with some success since the middle of July. By the end of August, **Totenkopf** and **Wiking** were fighting in front of Warsaw, halting the Russians at the Vistula. Into October, the two divisions were involved in fighting off fierce enemy attacks in front of the city and, less gloriously, putting down a rebellion inside it. By the end of that month, the pressure had eased to the point that 4.SS-Panzer-Korps was again pulled out of line into reserve.

In the West there was no such lull. While the armored SS divisions were behind the lines undergoing refit, the Allies brought the war directly to them. Having arrived at Arnhem on 7 September, **2.SS-Panzer-Korps** took up positions around that city. On 14 September, Hohenstaufen was ordered back into

Germany to ease reinforcement. That move had just begun, when the war virtually dropped in the laps of **Hohenstaufen** and **Frundsberg** in the form of the 1st British Airborne Division and "Operation Market-Garden." What followed was 12 days of house to house fighting as the intended Allied sweep across the Rhein faltered. Montgomery had intended Arnhem to be relieved in three days. Yet on the twelfth day, 2.SS-Panzer-Korps was mopping the last pockets of resistance East of the Rhein as the Allies finally closed the river from the West. Having been interupted at the beginning of their refit period, the divisions of **2. SS-Panzer-Korps** were now split up and sent to the rear to continue the process. **Frundsberg** was dispatched to the vicinity of Geilenkirchen. **Hohenstaufen** reformed the corps with **Das Reich** in the Schnee-Eifel.

With the failure of "Market-Garden", Hitler considered that the Allies were in a vulnerable position. He perceived, or thought he did, that the enemy's lines were overextended and too lightly held in the Ardennes. That site was also attractive because it was the location of the dramatic breakthrough in 1940. Perhaps it would work again. The plan was to push through the weakly held Ardennes Front, drive on the Meuse and beyond, toward Antwerp. If that port could be captured, the British-Canadian 21st Army Group would be trapped, cut off from supply and forced into a second, larger, even more disastrous Dunkirk.

The plan had some chance of success, although slight, and if successful would certainly ease the pressure in the West for months to come. But for success, a number of conditions had to be met, among them, suppression of Allied air superiority, sufficient fuel supply and rapid "Blitzkrieg" like movement. These conditions were not to be fulfilled. The Luftwaffe simply could not challenge Allied mastery in the skies. Fog did ground enemy planes for a few days, but once that lifted, the SS Armor found itself extremely vulnerable to P-47s and Typhoons. Fuel supply proved inadequate, so much so that on a number of occasions tactically favorable moves had to be foregone in the search for Allied fuel dumps. But, perhaps most serious, the leadership of the "Blitzkrieg" days was not there. Guderian and Manstein had been replaced by Dietrich and Peiper. Even the

Hitler Jugend

A still from some well-known movie footage, showing Panther ausf As of HJ moving through Caen on D-Day. The building in the background which is frequently cropped off, identifies the exact location of this shot. [Bundesarchiv]

best of the SS commanders, Hausser and Steiner, were not present.

Of "Sepp" Dietrich, who had risen from command of the tiny "Stabswache" to leadership of 6.Panzer-Armee, Baron von der Heydte, commander of German paratroop forces for the Ardennes offensive said:

> He had all the qualities of a first-class NCO of the old German Army; he was personally brave, tough and disciplined and he cared for his men as though they were children....He was feared, respected, and even loved, but he was certainly not a commander.

And further, he was drinking; never drunk, but not quite sober. When he gave orders, they were frequently imprecise. Among the orders that he gave his point troops was a particularly ambivalent one; "No time is to be wasted in the matter of prisoners". To von der Heydte this meant that any captured enemy soldiers were to be disarmed and left for following troops. To Peiper, it meant something quite different. Obersturmbannführer Joachim Peiper was 28 years old, handsome and brave, and utterly ruthless. He had gained a reputation for leading successful, if quite costly, counterattacks during the fierce defensive fighting on the Eastern Front. To Peiper and to the men of Kampfgruppe Peiper, the armored battlegroup of "LAH" entrusted with the task of leading the breakthrough to the Meuse, Dietrich's order meant license to treat captured enemy troops as they would have in the East. There, prisoners were often not taken. Before the offensive fizzled out at the end of the year, Peiper's men would be guilty of a number of attrocities, most notably the massacre of 86 US prisoners at Malmedy.

Four of the six SS armored divisions that had fought at Normandy were assigned to 6. Panzer-Armee for the Ardennes offensive. **LAH** and **HJ** of **1. SS-Panzer-Korps** were assigned to the first wave of the planned assault. On 16 December 1944, they were to punch through the lines held by green US divisions, for which task they were given considerable extra armor. **Das Reich** and **Hohenstaufen** [**2. SS-Panzer-Korps**] were held back in reserve, to be released to continue the advance if the first was slowed. The SS divisions were given the Northern and shorter route to the Meuse. They had ten miles less to cover (48 vs. 58) than the six Wehrmacht Panzer divisions assigned to the attack.

The offensive opened on 16 December, with less than overwhelming success. **HJ**, in particular, was halted along its entire front. **Leibstandarte**, especially **K-Gr Peiper**, had more luck, breaking through and starting to exploit to the West. 72

An SdKfz 251/7 engineer's vehicle of HJ complete with bridging equipment, is seen here under heavy foliage camouflage, halted by the side of a French road. Note the Black numerals which have been oversprayed, and the divisional insignia. [National Archives]

hours later **HJ** was still being held up, **LAH** was 20 miles to the West and out of fuel.

Hitler's offense was in a shambles. At this point, several days earlier than planned, **Hohenstaufen** was committed to the fight around Poteau, where parts of the US 7th Armored Division had been holding up the Southern sector of advance by **Leibstandarte**. The next day, 20 December, saw **HJ** swung South in an attempt to outflank the US positions, with no more success than before. On the same day **Das Reich** was committed, again much earlier than planned and not on the SS front which was stalled, but on the front of the Army's 560. Volkgrenadier Division at Samree to the South. By the 23rd, **HJ** was pulled out of line after being bled white, having pushed a grand total of seven miles into US lines. K-Gr Peiper, which had been stalled at Stoumont, first by lack of fuel and then by US resistance since the 19th, and cut off since the 21st, was given permission to abandon its vehicles and pull back. **Hohenstaufen** had reached Salmchateau, the farthest point of advance on the SS Front, but was now stalled still less than halfway to the Meuse. **Das Reich** was the only SS division still moving. Attacking repeatedly to the North in the direction of Huy, attempting to regain the original SS line of advance, it was forced Westward and eventually halted by a scratch force of US Armored Divisions. The Americans held the high ground north of the Marche-Manay road against the German attacks for six days. On the 25th **Das Reich** took Manay, but was unable to advance beyond. The next day the attack was to the West, and the following day, having been reinforced by **Hohenstaufen** and a grenadier regiment from **HJ**, at Erezee another five miles Westward. On 29 December, after a final unsuccessful thrust on the road to Hotton, the attack was called off. The remainder of **HJ** and **LAH**, which had been directed against Bastogne on the 27th, were now joined by the formations retreating from the West.

New Year found the four divisions which had been involved in the Ardennes operation assembled around Bastogne, making the final assaults on the town and trying to halt the move to Patton's Third Army up from the South. All had paid a price for their attacks, **HJ** was less than half strength, but none would be allowed the time to rest and refit. Crises were developing elsewhere that needed the attention of this once potent spearhead of the Third Reich.

The new year found the military situation deteriorating on all fronts. In the West, the failure of the Ardennes Offensive left the Germans in a weakened condition all along the front. Units that had been shorted on men and equipment to provide the extra punch for the spearhead divisions, now had to face Allied counterattacks. And those which had taken part in the offensive had taken losses which could no longer be made good. **Frundsberg** near Aachen and **GvB** in the Saar had seen some fighting, but were in much better condition than the four around Bastogne. **RFSS** was still falling back in Italy, but the most serious problem had developed in Hungary. There, in mid-December, a Russian offensive had trapped **Florian Geyer** and the rest of **9.SS-Korps** (the incomplete **22. SS-Kav-Div.** and the Army's Feldherrnhalle and 13. PanzerDiv) in Budapest.

The first reaction was to use SS divisions to free the trapped SS Corps. The first to be moved to Hungary was **4. SS-Panzer-Korps**, **Totenkopf** and **Wiking**, which had been spending a relatively quiet two months behind the Vistula bridgehead in Poland. This move was to prove disastrous as the German line in front of Warsaw collapsed under Russian attacks immediately after they were pulled out. **4.SS-Panzer-Korps** had been the only reserve on that front. When the Russian attack was finally halted on the Oder, the enemy was almost within sight of Berlin. And most tragically, these last sound SS divisions were wasted in the attack on Budapest.

Hitler's pride declared that the Hungarian capital must be held. Yet had a link up been achieved, it wouldn't have helped the overall German position in any way. The Allies must have been pleased to find that Hitler's best divisions were bogged down on what can only be called a minor front, while the German homeland was about to be invaded from both sides. They did not even succeed in relieving the city. Having gotten as close as the airport on 11 January 1945, **Totenkopf** was inexplicably sent on a pointless move around the North of the city, never getting as close again. By the end of the month, they were being driven towards the Southwest in some disorder by powerful Russian counterattacks. Not only had Budapest not been relieved but 4.SS-Panzer-Korps was in dire shape. But rather than accept the loss of Hungary and pull all useable troops out, at the end of January Hitler insisted upon another counterattack to regain the lost territory, aimed again at linking up with Budapest. In pursuit of this hopeless task, SS divisions were pulled away from the West, where they formed the only significant reserve. The results were predictable. Instead of being in position to contest the Allied Rhein crossing, they were in Hungary wasting their last strength on a false hope.

After the failure in the Ardennes, the SS divisions that had been involved were pulled back to refit areas. They were not to remain there long enough to achieve much. On 10 January **Leibstandarte** had been pulled back from Bastogne, being posted to the Bonn area. **HJ**, at about the same time, had been moved from Bastogne to the west of Koln. Both divisions, on about the 20th, were ordered to proceed to the area north of Budapest where the Russians had broken through across the Hron River. In a series of attacks beginning 5 February, they were successful in forcing the enemy back to the East bank. At the beginning of February, **Das Reich** followed a similar pattern, being pulled from Bastogne at the end of January and moved almost immediately to the area West of Budapest to which the divisions of **4.SS-Panzer-Korps** had been forced by enemy pressure. All this activity, however, failed to achieve its primary objective, saving the encircled **9.SS-Korps** in Budapest. On 12 February the defense of the city collapsed. Of the 50,000 men who were trapped in the city two months before, only 800 broke through the German lines (and only 170 of them were SS).

The end of February 1945 saw the last desperate moves by a confused and overwhelmed German High Command. **Frundsberg** which had been roughly handled in three months of hard fighting near Aachen, in the Saar and near Strasburg, was nevertheless transferred to Pomerania East of the Oder facing the Russians. No sooner had it taken position that it was brushed aside by the massive Russian attacks of early March. Likewise **Hohenstaufen**, after hard fighting around Houfalize in which most of its remaining equipment was lost, was hastily transferred to the East in early March in a futile attempt to shore up the collapsing position in Hungary. The net effect of these moves from West to East had been to weaken the West without helping the East. The four SS armored divisions in Hungary, instead of being withdrawn to bolster the German positions in Western Poland, were launched on 6 March on a last, futile offensive aimed again at Budapest.

The attack, was code named "Fruhlingserwachen" (Morning Watch), from the northshore of the Plattensee toward the Danube. After some initial success, the offensive ground to a halt, stopped by mud and stubborn Russian resistance. The last ounce having been wrung from these tired formations, all that remained was retreat, back to Vienna, and when that couldn't be held, further North and West.

And inevitably there was the surrender as one by one they passed into captivity; **LAH**, **HJ**, **RFSS**, **Hohenstaufen** and **Totenkopf** in Austria, **Das Reich**, **Frundsberg** and **Wiking** in Czechoslovakia, **Prinz Eugen** in the Balkans; **GvB** in Southeastern Germany; and **Nordland** in Berlin itself. No matter how they might have been employed, ultimately these divisions could not have stemmed the overwhelming flood of Allied and Russian power that broke over the failing Third Reich. In that last year they rapidly became mere shadows of their former strength, reflecting now only from a great distance the glory they had once believed to be theirs.

The men who fought the battles at Normandy, winning and losing, and some dying. [Above] Three grenadiers of HJ, looking very boyish now, are in the hands of Canadian troops, having been captured at Carpiquet airfield, 4 July 1944. Note the mix-and-match camouflage patterns of their uniforms. There was no standardization of dress at this stage of the conflict. [Public Archives Canada] [Left] The other side of the coin, a group of GIs are glumly awaiting transfer to a POW camp, guarded by two Das Reich soldiers in the vincinity of Carentan. [Below] The ultimate price, an Unterscharführer of Leibstandarte, left behind in Falaise, was flushed out and killed by advancing Canadian troops, 16 August. [Public Archives Canada]

Three views of the retreat across France. Not surprisingly, these photographs are increasingly of Allied origin as the Germans were too busy to document their disasters. [Above] A Sherman of Patton's Third Army moves to exploit the break-through West of St. Lo. On its way it passes two abandoned PzKpfw IV ausf Js of Das Reich. This division and HJ were among the last SS divisions to continue using divisional markings on their vehicles. Note the faintly visible, probably Yellow, Kampfrune on the left rear plate of both tanks. [US Army] [Left] An SdKfz 251/9 support SPW and a StuG III ausf G of Das Reich are being inspected by a Canadian soldier where they were abandoned at Elbeuf. It was here at the Seine that the last efforts were made to prevent the loss of all of France. And it was here that Das Reich lost the last of its vehicles. [Public Archives Canada] [Below] An M7 Priest passes the last resting place of Iron Cross winner, Unterscharführer Josef Richtfeld. There must have been enough time to produce the elaborate fence around his grave site before his division, GvB, was forced again into retreat. [US Army]

The war in the East continued with the same disastrous result. In Poland, the Germans were continually pushed back in spite of the best efforts of Wiking and Totenkopf. [Above & Left] Two views of Wiking Panthers moving across the flatlands of East Prussia and Western Poland. [Bundesarchiv] [Below] A rare shot of rarely seen troops, SS-Fallschirmjäger, only a few regiments of which were raised late in the war. While some had received jump training, they were never used in their intended role. Passing in the background is a StuG III ausf G. Note the late-style return rollers. [Bundesarchiv]

In the North, Nordland fought against overwhelming odds and fell back again and again. [Right] Two Hetzers of Nordland move back into combat, being ridden by troopers of Fallschirmjäger-Rgt 25. [Center] Vielfachwerferbatterie 521, attached to Nordland, employed a hybrid vehicle, Opel Maultiers with captured Russian Katyusha rocket launchers. The armored halftracks are painted Sand Yellow with a heavy overspray of Olive Green.

Nordland

The last Winter of the war in the East found Wiking in Hungary hoping to stop one more Russian thrust. These vehicles are in overall Sand Yellow. Supplies of White paint never made their way to the troops this last winter. An interesting column of vehicles can be seen here. Next to the Kfz 1 VW Kubelwagen is a column of light APCs. The first two are late model SdKfz 250/1 ISPWs followed by an SdKfz 250/9 ISPW [2 cm] with a light armored car turret. To the left is a column of Maultier halftrack lorries. [Bundesarchiv]

Operation "Market-Garden" dropped the British 1st Airborne Division into Arhhem and in the midst of 2.SS-Panzer-Korps. Montgomery's plans went wrong from the beginning. Instead of the three days it was supposed to take the Allied ground forces to reach the Rhein and link up with the paratroopers, it took 12, by which time the 1st Airborne had been overwhelmed. [Above] Three grenadiers of Hohenstaufen were happy to relieve the two Red Devils in the back of their Willys MB Jeep. The vehicle is entirely as it landed by glider, in overall Olive Drab with British markings. [Bundesarchiv] [Right] Driving their way into the city, StuG IIIs of Hohenstaufen pass their own casualties from earlier in the battle.

"Das Reich" ---------
K-Gr "Peiper" ("LAH") _____
Main Body "LAH" ....
"HJ" ---..---..---..---
"Hohenstaufen" ---.----.----.----
Enemy Attacks ◁
Major Battle ✂

The Ardennes offensive was Hitler's last gamble in the West, one with some chance of success. But there were too many ifs. For a few days, the Germans were able to advance well in some places, but fuel and the weather brought those first victorious thrusts to a standstill. [Above] A company command group of K-Gr Peiper, dismounted from their late-model SdKfz 250 ISPW, inspects a crossroad between Malmedy and St. Vith. Note that the impracticality of trying to tuck the heavy camouflage pants into the short late-war issue boats has led to the habit of wearing the pants unbloused. [Left] Appearing more than a year older since we last saw him, Standartenführer Joachim Peiper, commander of the armored spearhead of the whole offensive, is seen here. [Below] Panzergrenadiers on top, another late-war vehicle is seen here. This time it is a Pz IV/70 Panzerjager of HJ. Note the nearly pristine condition of the ambush scheme paint job. [US Army]

Another rare view of a rare late war vehicle. Being the first to receive new equipment as it came into service, SS units were frequently the only ones to receive some just-developed vehicles. In this case it is an SdKfz 234/1 Tatra "tropical" armored car. This shot must be from the first days of the campaign as it shows the eight wheel carrying a load of still smiling HJ grenadiers. [US Army]

A motorcyclist of HJ delivers a message to some Luftwaffe Fallschirmjäger who are riding an HJ Tiger ausf B King Tiger. Of interest is the evidence of the carefully sprayed ambush scheme visible on the rear of the Tiger II. Also the U-boat leathers being worn by the motorcyclist. This was a much more appropriate use for this all leather suit than as a tanker's uniform. [US Army]

The Last Offensive:
Hungary, January-March 1945

An SS trooper is seen discussing the world situation with a disarmed Hungarian. There is little reason for them to smile. This photo is believed to be from one of the last series of propaganda shots attempting to show German strength. It was probably taken at Stuhlweissenburg [Szekesfehervar] west of Budapest, just prior to the last offensive, Unternehmen Frühlingserwachen [Morning Watch]. The Tiger II in the background is not an SS vehicle, although it may belong to an associated Army sPz-Abt.

Having withdrawn all the way from Oranienbaum to Berlin, Nordland fought its last battles around the grave of its Führer. It died too. Among the last of its vehicles, this late SdKfz 250/1 ISPW is seen in the streets of Berlin. It was painted overall Sand Yellow with a hasty Red Brown overspray and a great deal of dirt. The division fought on for a few more days, surrendering in Charlottenberg, just West of the city.

Other Waffen-SS troops ended the war as victims of the outrage that followed discovery of the system of atrocities they had aided. Here can be seen the bodies of grenadiers of a detached battalion of Wiking which had taken over the defense of KL Dachau in Bavaria from camp guards. When the defenders of such camps surrendered, those who had not been killed in the battle were frequently executed by the Allies or turned over to the justice of the ex-prisoners. There were few survivors.

A fitting final shot. A Kfz 70, probably a Steyr 1500A of Hitlerjugend **burns by the side of a French road. That fire marks the end of a system that witnessed great glory and committed atrocious horrors. And it marks the end of the fighting units of the Waffen-SS that were to the world the symbol of its armed strength.** [Bundesarchiv]

POLAND

Charlottenberg
"Nordland" ★ • BERLIN

Dresden ★ Part of
"Das Reich"

GERMANY

PRAQUE ★ Part of "Das Reich"

CZECHOSLOVAKIA

Schonau ★ "Frundsberg"

Maissau ★ "Totenkopf"

Surrender Positions:
May 1945

VIENNA •

Linz • ★ "HJ"
Enns

Positions indicate location of
mass of division. Detached
and support units not shown.

Steyr ★ "LAH"
"Hohenstaufen"

MUNICH •

"GvB"
★
Kreuth

AUSTRIA

"Wiking"
★
Furstenfeld

• Innsbruck

"RFSS"
★
Klagenfurt

YUGOSLAVIA

ITALY